WHY DO I KEEP DOING THIS?

Also by Kati Morton

Are u ok?: A Guide to Caring for Your Mental Health

Traumatized: Identify, Understand, and Cope with PTSD and Emotional Stress

Unlearn the Habits Keeping You Stuck and Unhappy

WHY DO I KEEP DOING THIS?

KATI MORTON

New York Boston

The tools and information presented herein are not intended to replace the services of trained health professionals or be a substitute for medical advice. You are advised to consult with your health care professional with regard to matters relating to your health, and in particular regarding matters that may require diagnosis or medical attention.

Details relating to the author's life are reflected faithfully to the best of their ability, while recognizing that others who were present might recall things differently. Names and identifying details have been changed to protect the privacy and safety of others, including clients who shared their stories for this book.

Balance
Hachette Book Group
1290 Avenue of the Americas
New York, NY 10104
GCP-Balance.com
@GCPBalance

First Edition: December 2025

Balance is an imprint of Grand Central Publishing. The Balance name and logo are registered trademarks of Hachette Book Group, Inc.

The publisher is not responsible for websites (or their content) that are not owned by the publisher.

The Hachette Speakers Bureau provides a wide range of authors for speaking events. To find out more, go to hachettespeakersbureau.com or email HachetteSpeakers@hbgusa.com.

Balance books may be purchased in bulk for business, educational, or promotional use. For information, please contact your local bookseller or the Hachette Book Group Special Markets Department at special.markets@hbgusa.com.

Library of Congress Cataloging-in-Publication Data has been applied for.

ISBNs: 978-0-306-83654-1 (paper over board), 978-0-306-83655-8 (ebook)

Printed in the United States of America

LSC-C

Printing 1, 2025

For anyone who, like me, has been exhausted from trying to hold it all together. Thinking we could keep everything under control if we just worked harder. I see you. I am you.

AUTHOR'S NOTE

THE PEOPLE AND PATIENTS I HAVE DISCUSSED IN THIS BOOK HAVE charitably given their permission. Many of the stories I share are very personal and come from those I know in my private life, as well as from my own life experience. To protect the privacy of those mentioned, all names and identifying details have been changed. The stories shared in this book are done to further illustrate how mental health and especially our urge to control can affect us. This book is meant to empower you to get the help you need and deserve. It is not a replacement for actual mental health treatment. If you are struggling with mental health issues, I urge you to seek professional help as soon as possible.

CONTENTS

WHY DO I KEEP DOING THIS?

Introduction

MANY OF US HAVE BEEN TOLD SINCE CHILDHOOD THAT WE NEED to keep it together, be less dramatic, or toughen up. Some of us were told not to cry, to stop making a scene, or that our emotions were too much. As we got older, our upsets were dismissed, labeled as overreactions, or even seen as embarrassing. The message was clear: Falling apart is a failure, and if we just tried harder, we could appear unfazed.

These toxic ideas teach us to stuff our feelings down, ignore our instincts, and worry more about how we're perceived than how we actually feel. We learn that our emotional reactions should be controlled. But here's the paradox: While controlling our emotions is seen as a strength, controlling others is condemned. A controlling friend or partner is toxic. Trying to manage someone indirectly is passive-aggressive. The very thing we are trained to do, keep things under control, becomes the thing that harms our relationships, our well-being, and, ultimately, ourselves.

Control is a precarious thing. It keeps us safe and in line, but it can also be the very thing that breaks us.

And I know this firsthand.

I have always needed things to be just right. As a kid, I believed that if I could be perfect, if I could anticipate what people needed, say the right things, and avoid mistakes, then everything would be okay. If I could control my environment, I could prevent problems before they happened. I didn't see this as control at the time. I thought I was being responsible, prepared, a good friend. But looking back, I realize that this constant need to manage everything wasn't just about doing my best, it was about trying to feel safe.

In 2023, I hit a breaking point. I had spent the year working relentlessly, convinced that if I just did more, I would finally feel accomplished. But no matter how much I did, it never felt like enough. I ignored my exhaustion, dismissed my own needs, and kept pushing forward. Taking a break felt like failure. Slowing down felt unsafe. So I kept going. Until one day, I realized I wasn't just burned out, I was resenting the very things I had once loved.

I snapped at my husband over something small. I felt irritated that my dog needed a walk. I was exhausted but refused to rest. And worst of all? I was annoyed with myself for feeling this way.

"Get it together, Kati," I told myself.

I knew I needed a break just to think straight, but I couldn't let myself take one. Every time I even considered stepping away, guilt kicked in. The fear of falling behind, of failing because of time off, made rest feel counterproductive. So I kept going. And going.

Until I finally sat down and started journaling about it.

That's when I saw the pattern.

It wasn't just about working too much or struggling to take breaks. It was something deeper, something I had been blind to for years. I wasn't just exhausted; I was trapped in an endless cycle of trying to control everything around me. My to-do lists, my emotions, my relationships—I was holding on so tightly that I didn't even realize how much I was suffocating myself.

And I was frustrated to find myself here again. Hadn't I already worked through all of this? I had been in therapy since I was fifteen, done the self-reflection, put in the work. When would I finally get over this feeling of not being enough? When would I stop running myself into the ground just to prove something, to myself, to others? And yet here I was, stuck in the same exhausting cycle.

Why did I keep doing this?

I had spent years believing that if I could just stay on top of everything, anticipate every problem, and work harder than everyone else, I would finally feel at peace. But instead, I felt more anxious, more disconnected, and more on edge than ever before. I was constantly managing, fixing, and adjusting, trying to orchestrate my world in a way that would prevent failure, rejection, or disappointment. And yet despite all of my efforts, those feelings still found me.

It wasn't just about control, it was about safety. Somewhere along the way, I had learned that control was my shield, my way of keeping chaos at bay. If I could manage everything perfectly, I could avoid pain. But the more I tried to control, the more out of control I felt. The harder I gripped, the more everything slipped through my fingers.

This realization wasn't just a professional one, it was deeply personal. As a therapist, I had spent years helping others untangle their struggles with anxiety, perfectionism, and self-sabotage. I had seen firsthand how control showed up in their lives, just as it had in mine. The need to be the best. The fear of making a mistake. The exhausting cycle of overworking, overapologizing, and overfunctioning, all in the hope that it would somehow make us feel enough.

And now, here I was, caught in the same trap.

That's why this book exists. Because I know I'm not the only one. I see it in my patients, my friends, and my online community. So many of us push ourselves to the brink, believing that if we just manage things better, try harder, and never let anything slip, we'll finally feel okay. But the truth is, control isn't saving us, it's breaking us.

That's what we're going to unpack in these pages. Why we keep doing this to ourselves, where it comes from, and, most importantly, how to finally let go in a way that doesn't feel like free-falling. Because there is another way, a way that allows us to feel safe, supported, and whole without needing to control every single detail of our lives.

I'm not here to tell you to simply "let go and trust the process." I know how terrifying that sounds. I know how impossible it feels when every instinct is telling you to hold on tighter. But I also know that there is freedom in learning to loosen our grip. There is peace in realizing that we don't have to carry everything alone.

If you've ever felt stuck in this cycle, you're not alone. And the good news? You don't have to stay here.

Let's dive in.

Chapter 1

CONTROL AND OUR UPBRINGING

How Our Family Dynamics Set the Tone

THE URGE TO CONTROL IS EVERYWHERE, AND MOST OF US CAN track it back to the way we were raised. If our parents struggled with addiction, it likely felt like everything was out of control, so we did our best to keep it all together, thinking that if they saw how hard we were working they would stop. If our dad traveled a lot for work, we might think that if we were perfect at school and in sports he would want to be home more often, and if our mom overate when things got stressful, we might think that was the best way to cope with our feelings. Almost no one grows up without experiencing some examples of attempted control. So much of our life is unpredictable and uncomfortable, and of course we want to do what we can to make it feel better.

And that's the first piece that is important to recognize. Wanting to control things is normal. Our nervous systems are wired to seek out any threat to our physical or emotional safety, and when something is unknown or unpredictable it can feel dangerous. Therefore, our brain and body get ready to take action, whether that action is to fight back or run away from the potential threat. Taking action is our way of reasserting our control over the situation.

When we are young, we don't have many options or resources to help us take action, so we often can't run away or arm ourselves in a way that feels better. Instead, we use what we have—our bodies—and we control that. This is what can lead to trying to be perfect, manipulating others into doing what we need, or even controlling what we eat. That's why our upbringing can have such an impact on how we engage with the world. It creates the blueprint for our relationships and our ways of coping with the unknown.

THE BLUEPRINT

If we grew up in a home where the love was inconsistent, or we were harmed for having needs and taking up space, it is going to be hard for us to know who to go to when we need comfort. This is because our parents help us create a blueprint for relationships and we accept it as fact because we don't know any other way. So if they were inconsistent or abusive, we will find other people who mimic those traits. Not because we like it or think our childhood was amazing, but because it's comfortable. We know what to expect, and, frankly, we think it's what we deserve. This is why we feel like we keep finding ourselves in the same relationship over and over, or at least feeling the same way when it ends.

I will always remember when my therapist pointed out the fact that all my ex-boyfriends seemed to put me second. She called my attention to this when my current boyfriend expected me to always come over to his apartment, and he hadn't even been to mine. I was frustrated, and complained to her that I was stressed about the amount of money I was spending on gas. That was the issue I came into my session with, my financial stress. She quickly realized that this problem I was having didn't have anything to do with money, but the fact that I had picked another boyfriend who didn't believe in balance or compromise. It was his way or the highway.

She recalled a few ex-boyfriends from the past and how they all seemed to not make time for me or not even make an effort to be with me. I felt like the wind was knocked right out of my sails. She was right. I kept thinking that relationships take work, and if I just tried harder, it would all come together. It took some time, and I had to overcome a lot of resistance, but I was able to realize that I was picking unavailable men. Men that I couldn't count on to show up for me, who would make plans only to cancel them at the last minute, and not pick up when I called. Without realizing it, I was picking men who kept leaving me hanging, expecting more, not knowing if or when they would show up for me. I was dating men who gave me the same feeling my dad did. It matched my blueprint.

I know it's cliché to pin an issue on a parent, but sometimes it fits. I don't do this to blame, but rather to understand. If we don't first know where this unhealthy pattern is coming from, we can't change it. Knowing that I was attracted to men who weren't available or consistent helped me realize that my picker wasn't properly calibrated. In fact, it was still stuck in the '90s and in need of an overhaul.

INTERNALIZING THE BLUEPRINT

I see this a lot in my patients and online community as well. Our parents weren't able to be there for us in a consistent way, and because we are children and don't understand the reasons behind it, we assume it's our fault. We internalize their unpredictability and assume that if we just did things better, were perfect, or were more like them, they would see us and show up for us. It's incredibly vital to a child's development to feel seen, heard, and understood. Without this, we can struggle to develop a solid foundation of trust in others and in ourselves.

Ruby, a member of my community, shared how when she was growing up both of her parents were high achievers, working away from home a lot, and placing a lot of emphasis on how well she did in school and sports. She hated when they would go away, but if she got good grades or won an award (i.e., controlled her conditions), when they got home they would all go out to dinner to celebrate. This was one of the few times when she got their undivided attention. I know we have given the word "attention" a bad reputation, but it's something we all need. Doing things for attention explains most of our behaviors as humans. We need other people around us, we need connection, and there isn't anything wrong with seeking it out.

Those dinners out were, and still are, some of Ruby's favorite memories because she felt seen, heard, and important. However, this changed the way she engaged with life going forward. She told me that she struggles with perfectionism, is a workaholic, and hasn't had a romantic relationship that lasted more than six months. She attributes these issues to the fact that she has always tied her self-worth to her work, and if she's not getting a promotion or being recognized for her efforts, then she feels like a failure. She works harder and harder and doesn't leave time for herself or her relationships. When she starts dating someone, if they are too available or give her too much attention, it scares her off. She's not used to regular attention or someone doting after her; she prefers to earn that kind of care. She's on a control superhighway.

As a result, the relationships she has been in are dismissive, unavailable, and difficult to connect with. She told me that her last boyfriend would disappear for weeks at a time because of his work, and after months of their being together, he still wouldn't call her his girlfriend. She thought she was in love and wanted to be exclusive... He broke up with her shortly thereafter.

I am not saying that we always pick people who remind us of our parents, but we do tend to be more attracted to people who are familiar and comfortable. That leaves less room for unpredictable behavior and can also mean they're only able to offer us the type of love we are used to getting.

Another member of my community, Tara, shared how she thought her family was perfect growing up. They went on family vacations and her mom stayed home with her and her three siblings while her dad worked in the city. She can't even remember a time when her parents fought and was blindsided when they told them they were getting a divorce. Tara was eleven years old.

This change meant that they had to sell the house she had grown up in and move into a smaller condo where she shared a room with her sister. Her dad was supposed to take them every weekend but would often just not show, later saying that something came up at work. Tara was so disappointed in her dad and how he had changed that she vowed to never put her children through something like that. She admitted that she only dates men who she feels need her and who constantly shower her with attention. She thought this would prevent her childhood experience from happening again.

Unfortunately, all this did was cause her to be in codependent relationships. She was fulfilled because she felt needed and that gave her a sense of security, and the men she dated required her support to keep them going. At first, she thought that was normal and things were exactly as they should be. It wasn't until years later and after she was married that she realized it wasn't healthy. She started to feel resentful of her husband for not being a self-starter, not earning as much money, and not helping out around the house. Sure, she had done all of those things for years, but wasn't he supposed to be her partner? Her friends' marriages didn't look like this. How did she end up here?

EXTERNAL FIXES

When we look out into the world hoping others will heal our wounds, we give all of our power away. We are at the mercy of other people and their desires, and this can make us feel helpless and hopeless. I hear this a lot in my community as well, like this comment from Taylor:

> *If my mom would just apologize to me for all of the pain she caused, then I could move on. She needs to admit what she did and make amends. Then I will be able to heal.*

By making our healing contingent upon someone else's actions, we are placing our happiness in their hands. I am not saying that others won't ever offer us the words we need, but they can't do that every time we need them to, and they aren't always going to know just what we need. The reason we keep trying to find someone who will give us all that we need is because it's human nature to look to others to soothe us. In fact, our nervous system is wired for that. Dr. Stephen Porges's research on polyvagal theory explains why connection is so vital to our psychological health. It's the reason that we are calmed as babies when our mother feeds us or rubs our back, why we feel so much better after talking with a close friend about an issue we are dealing with. Connection with others is soothing to us, and so it's natural that we would seek it out as a way of feeling better about ourselves.

The problem isn't in the connections or in our need for others, it's in our inability to do it alone and in our efforts to control people and situations. Much of our ability to soothe ourselves comes from watching our parents do it themselves, and unfortunately, they don't always know how to. In the same way we pass down family recipes and genetic traits, we also share our ways of coping with the world. Emotional regulation skills aren't something that's taught in school, and our older generations probably haven't even heard of that term, which makes it impossible for them to teach it to us. It's more likely that we watched our parents stuff down their emotions, drink to cope, or fly into a rage when things didn't go their way.

They never showed us what to do when we were struggling or offered us ideas of how to process through the difficult moments. All we know is that it feels better when other people comfort us, and so we go looking for someone to make it all better. While that can feel good from time to time, there can also be times when this strategy hurts us and we are left feeling worse. People let us down, have their own lives to tend to, and cannot be available when we need them. This can reinforce the belief that we aren't good enough, not worthy of love.

RECALIBRATION

Breaking out of an unhealthy pattern sounds so simple. I don't like the way I am thinking or acting, so I am going to think and act in a different way. Ta-da! But it's much more complicated. These patterns aren't new. We have usually been acting in these ways for most of our life, and we don't always know another way of behaving. It would be like asking someone sneezing to stop halfway through. It feels physically impossible. Which is why I prefer to figure out where these patterns are coming from, what story they are connected to, and where I see these types of behaviors most.

Figuring out the origin sounds simple enough, but it really takes honesty and challenging some beliefs we've had about our upbringing. So often I will hear from my community that they love their parents and had the best childhood, so they don't think that has anything to do with how they are acting. It's not that we are trying to blame our upbringing for everything going wrong in our life, but it does help to look back on the relationship dynamics we grew up with and see if any of that is feeding into our issues now. Meaning that we could have had a great relationship with our mom, but if we honestly consider the relationship, we realize that neither of us were ever comfortable with conflict. All of our memories are happy and great because it wasn't okay for it to be any other way. This could explain why having a fight with a friend causes us to pull away or assume the relationship is over. We never learned how to disagree and then come together again.

We need to remember that doing this kind of personal research and assessment isn't so that we have someone to blame, it's so we can stop acting in ways that upset us. Just like we can tell ourselves unhelpful stories about who we are and what we want, we can also have fabricated positive stories that everything was great and our family was perfect. It's important for us to see our past without any filters or defensiveness. Just like Justin from my community shared:

> "*I always thought my family was good—not perfect, but good enough. I had an okay childhood and my parents did their best. It wasn't until my first marriage was falling apart that I realized I didn't know how to fight without completely losing my shit. I would call her names, scream at her, and say things I wish I could take back. When we tried family therapy to work through this, I realized the impact it was having on my kids, and suddenly it hit me. I was doing what my parents did. Someone was always yelling in my home, and I often felt like I had to scream to be heard at all. This type of communication was all I knew. I just wish I had realized this wasn't healthy years before I did. Maybe then I could have saved my marriage.*

It can be hard for us to look back and see things clearly and without bias. It's human nature to want to protect those we love. Not to mention that when we look back, we are looking at a situation with everything we know now, not what we were aware of back then. Which means that things we may think are obvious now weren't so obvious when we were a child.

PAST STORIES

Once we know where these thoughts and behaviors are coming from, we can work to figure out the story we told ourselves about it. Taking Justin's example, we can see that he believed he had to scream to be heard and may have told himself that it was the only way to get attention or love. The story could be that relationships require force, and that's not only how we get the love and attention we need but also how we show it to others. I know that may sound strange to those of us who didn't grow up in that environment, but we all have stories we tell ourselves to make sense of our surroundings. The trick is identifying them.

One way I have worked on this was to take one of my most bothersome thoughts, like my belief that I have to earn love by being perfect, and be curious (not judgmental) about it. A trick we use in therapy to get us moving in the right direction is to use what is known as "downward arrow technique." In short, it helps us identify why we act and feel the way we do. In this case it would work like this:

If the thought is, "I have to work hard to get love and attention."

Then the first question is, "What does having to work hard for love and attention say about you?"

Answer: "That I am not worthy of love and attention without working hard."

Question: "If that were true, what would that mean?"

Answer: "That just being myself isn't enough."

Question: "If that were true, what would that mean?"

Answer: "That I am not enough."

Obviously, that's a shortened version, and it can take us some time to come up with those answers, but the goal is to figure out that core belief—in my case, that I am not enough. That final answer is the story I've been telling myself all these years and the reason my control presents in competitive, perfectionistic, and people-pleasing ways. This story is what motivates the behaviors bothering me and the people I am in relationships with. Knowing this helps me better understand and even feel some compassion for myself. I don't believe that I am enough, and I have spent most of my life trying to prove that I am.

BABY STEPS

Next, we need to figure out what relationships or situations trigger this response in the smallest way. I know you may be surprised that I am starting with the least triggering, but it's easier to start with something small and work our way up. In my case this small thing could be that I don't like how much I apologize when things don't quite go as planned. I say "sorry" for things that didn't have anything to do with me, for being in someone's way, and even for taking up space in a shared environment. It's annoying and I hate it.

Just because this is small or sounds simple doesn't mean it's easy. Years ago, my therapist asked me to try not to say "sorry" when I couldn't explain what I was sorry for. Let's just say I failed week after week for months. While a behavior like apologizing too much may be easy to notice, the real challenge is doing the homework to change that behavior. Other common behaviors I have worked on with patients are things like asking for clarification rather than making assumptions, to stop constantly seeking validation, and to stop replaying past conversations. You will be surprised how many of your bothersome habits are born out of a core belief of not being enough and present in ways to control yourself and others.

The thing to remember is that even though we don't like some of the things we think or do, that doesn't mean we need to shame and blame ourselves for doing it. We didn't always get to choose the experiences we were subjected to or the people we had as role models. We took what we saw and learned from it, and that's all we are trying to do now. The fact that you are even reading this book and wanting to change is a huge step. We can't move forward if we keep getting in our own way, continuing to tell ourselves how unworthy we are, and then using whatever control tactics we learned worked as a child. We can learn from our past, respect it for what it was, and choose to do it differently tomorrow.

"WHY DO I KEEP DOING THIS?" EXERCISE— *QUESTIONS TO START THAT INTERNAL RESEARCH:*

1. What was your relationship with your father like? How do you feel about it as you reflect back?
2. What was your relationship with your mother like? How do you feel about it as you reflect back?
3. What types of patterns do you see in your relationships? Certain types of people? Did they all end for similar reasons? Do you keep looking for the same things?
4. How do you react when you don't feel accepted? Has that changed as you've gotten older?
5. Do you think love is something that has to be earned? Why or why not? Did you learn that yourself or did someone else teach it to you?
6. What are your beliefs about needing and getting attention? Where do you think those beliefs came from?

Chapter 2

PERFECTIONISM AND FEELING LIKE YOU'RE NOT ENOUGH

When Love Has to Be Earned

PERFECTIONISM MIGHT BE ONE OF THE MOST RECOGNIZABLE forms of control, at least from the outside. That person who is so obsessed with their grades that even an A-minus feels like death. Or the person who rewrites an email to their boss multiple times because they want to get it "right." We look at these examples, and we can see the need for control so clearly. But perfection is a fickle concept. In many ways we might feel like we should do things perfectly because if we really care about something and want to be proud of our accomplishments, why not do it "perfectly"? But on the other hand, we logically know that perfection isn't achievable and often leads to us feeling worse about ourselves in the end. Regardless of all of that, somewhere deep inside we still feel like we can make it happen. We try to control the outcome by pushing ourselves, striving to be the best, and even holding firm to the belief that once we finally reach perfection, we will be happy.

Everywhere we look, people are trying to tell us what we need to change about ourselves in order to get that job, boyfriend or girlfriend, or success in life. This is a great marketing ploy, because if we think we have a deficiency in an area and a product can fix it, then we are more likely to purchase that product. And many of us believe that we have to earn love and attention, that it's not something that's freely given. That something being given without earning it is suspect, not to be trusted, or must be a mistake. As a result, we convince ourselves that we need to change or control something about ourselves to finally achieve what we want.

EARNING OUR WORTH

My dad always traveled a lot for work, and because I didn't understand why he couldn't make it to all of my games and musical events, I thought it was because I wasn't good enough. I thought that if I got better grades or made the varsity team he would feel compelled to come and support me. I started working my butt off in school and sports, and became incredibly competitive, even against my friends. It wasn't until I slide-tackled a friend of mine during a soccer game that I realized I didn't like who I was becoming, but I didn't know how to change, either.

In order to break this competitive pattern I thought I had to stop "fighting to win" all the time. So I started trying to let other people win. My therapist at the time quickly told me that that wasn't the goal. She didn't care if I won or lost (I know, rude), she only cared what my thoughts about it were. She asked me to journal about what came up when I lost versus when I won something, and to focus on how that affected me. It was hard and I didn't understand what she was getting at. But since I am a people-pleaser, I got started and attempted another tactic to change my behavior. This time I tried to not care about the outcome, but that didn't feel honest, because deep down I still really wanted to win.

After weeks of going nowhere and getting frustrated, I suddenly had an epiphany while journaling. I was approaching this from the wrong angle. It was never about winning a game; it was always about getting attention and feeling like I had to earn it. In other words, I felt like I had to hustle for my worth, and if I wasn't hustling, how would I know when I had worked hard enough to justify receiving love? Instead of focusing on the symptoms of being overly competitive, my therapist was more interested in the drive behind it. She was pushing me to recognize my need for attention and the ways I was trying to control my outcomes to get it.

NEVER ENOUGH

You might wonder why that is. Why don't we believe that we are enough? The most common cause of this belief system is childhood trauma. I know "trauma" can sometimes feel like a strong word. Many in my community have shared how they don't think what they went through was actually traumatic, and by calling it that they think they are being dramatic. But know that in order for us to be traumatized we only have to experience something upsetting and stressful enough that we can't process it. We become overwhelmed by it and do our best to make sense of the hurtful situations. In short, trauma is more common than we realize. Not feeling safe or secure growing up could leave scars that make us question our worth and our place in the world. When we grow up being punished without reason, or harmed by those who are supposed to care for us, we can start to think that something is wrong with us. We must have done something to deserve this treatment, or if we had just acted in a better way it wouldn't have happened.

Having inconsistencies in our childhood could also cause us to strive for perfection and question our own worth. I know that's where my urges come from: always believing that my dad's absence had to do with my mediocrity and imperfections, and if I could just do better he would stay home more. Trying as hard as I could to prove that I was worth coming home for. Controlling everything I did so it was "perfect."

You see, as children we don't have a lot of resources or knowledge. We can't see outside of ourselves and our environment, so we often try to make sense of things by blaming ourselves. After all, it's the only thing we have complete control over. Just like I used to think that if I got perfect grades and was the best on my sport teams, my dad would suddenly be able to show up for them. I didn't understand that his work schedule had nothing to do with me or my behavior. I assumed that his absence was due to something I did or didn't do.

When our childhood is riddled with these upsets, we can feel from a young age that we are not good enough and spend the rest of our lives trying to prove that we are. This pushes us toward perfectionism. We can feel that we need to be nice to everybody at all times, that we have to take on more work or responsibility than others or apologize for everything we do, whether it was wrong or not. By doing so, our feelings of inadequacy will be soothed. But that's not how perfection works. We can't try harder than others and automatically feel better or complete something without mistakes and then feel like we are perfect. We end up trying to keep this act up, always striving for the best outcome, continuing to work harder day after day, because perfection is always just out of reach.

If you asked a hundred people how they would know if they were doing something perfectly, you would get a hundred different answers. In fact, that answer may even shift for some people depending on the day you asked them. It's elusive and amorphous, which is what makes it so desirable. If it was easy to achieve, then we wouldn't place any value in it.

STUCK ON REPEAT

I recently read in Julia Cameron's book *The Artist's Way*, "Perfection is not a quest for the best. It is a pursuit of the worst in ourselves."[1] That simple statement left me reeling. She was right. In my own efforts toward perfection I inadvertently highlighted all the ways in which I did something wrong. Ways in which I am wrong. I wasn't getting better at things or becoming the perfect daughter, I was just feeling worse about myself.

If this sounds familiar, here's something that has helped me: Instead of asking, "Did I do this perfectly?" I ask, "Did this move me forward?"

Progress, not perfection.

It's a small shift, but it interrupts the cycle. Instead of measuring my worth by impossible standards, I try to focus on whether I am learning, growing, or even just showing up. Some days, simply trying is enough.

Unfortunately, as I grew up these behaviors didn't change. I still felt like I had to earn love and attention. Even though my urge for perfection may have started in childhood, I continued to harm myself with it. The stories I created in my head when I was growing up are the ones that I still repeat to myself today. Even though I have more resources and knowledge now, I can still get stuck in this loop. I can still stand in my own way, blocking any progress and sabotaging myself. And that's because we need to understand how control manifests itself as perfectionism.

I remember when I was around ten or so years old, I went with my brother to a comic book shop to sell some of his comics. He wanted to buy one that was more expensive, and to afford to do that, he had to sell some first. While the woman at the store was looking over his comics, he pointed out all the flaws in each book. This one had a folded corner, this one a water stain, and the binding of this other one was a bit damaged. My brother needed the money from those comic books to get the one he really wanted, but he kept pointing out all the reasons why he shouldn't get that money from her.

That's what we do when we strive for perfection. We want something better, more successful, more valuable, but instead we end up pointing out all the flaws in our plan, the reasons we aren't worthy of it.

We strive to control our life, make everything perfect, all the while not believing we deserve it. If we get close, if we really try for something, our fear that we aren't good enough causes us to sabotage our progress. I hear stories like this every day, like this one from Holly. She shared:

> *I always wanted to have a boyfriend who truly cared. Checked in on me, and couldn't wait to see me again. I wanted a love story. Then I finally met Carson. He was kind, thoughtful, and always planned the most fun things for us to do. I was so in love with him, but I couldn't stop thinking that he was cheating on me or didn't love me as much as I loved him. This consumed me. I would call and text constantly, ask for him to tell me why he loves me, and I needed nonstop reminders of his affection. After a few months of this he broke up with me, and I was devastated. Looking back it's almost like I caused this myself, I made him leave me because I didn't believe I deserved his love. So I proved that to myself. It's the worst feeling.*

That's the thing about perfection and worth. Even if we believe that we want it to be perfect, we can also believe that we don't deserve it. In my life I have always thought that being perfect would garner me the attention and affection I craved, but the truth is that no amount of outside praise or affection could fix an internal problem.

What I really needed was to offer myself the love and attention I required, not look outward hoping someone else would do it for me.

OLD PATTERNS AND FEARS

Fighting our way out of old patterns sucks. As a therapist, I know better, but still act in ways that are childish, manipulative, and often hurtful. Those old beliefs are hard to quiet and when I am run-down it can feel like I don't even have a choice. But I do know that there are things we can do to try better, feel better, and be better to one another. Understanding is always where I start when I know I am acting out of line. I have gotten into the habit of asking myself questions when I journal. This may sound odd, because if I knew the answer why wouldn't I just do that and move on, right? Well, it's not always that easy. My working memory, or the things I can easily access, isn't representative of my full knowledge of my environment and self. It's just what I use the most, and that can be bad sometimes. For me to think in a different way I have started pondering it on paper, letting my brain pull up possible answers until I feel that one fits.

For example, when I was trying to figure out why I am so competitive and feel this urge to earn love I asked myself, "Why did you feel so jealous when that person did it better than you?" My automatic response was that it was because it was important to me and I wanted to feel seen. So I dug a little deeper and asked, "Why is feeling unseen by people so upsetting?" Which was honestly hard to answer, but I wrote that it was because if they don't see me, then do I exist? Ugh. It's through this kind of probing that I was able to discover that in my mind if someone wins something, that means that I lose, and that leaves me feeling completely lost and unimportant.

I know it won't always be that straightforward; most times it isn't. I have been in therapy off and on since I was fifteen and it's still difficult. But one thing I do know is that we all have the answers we seek, we just don't always know how to get to them. Being open to learning about ourselves instead of assuming we know it all helps and allows us to change and grow. Once we understand where our urge to control comes from, we can look for patterns. As a therapist, this is something I do all the time with my patients, but it's completely different to do it for ourselves. The reason I mention patterns is because doing something once doesn't mean anything. We can all act out of character one time, do something we regret, or date someone inappropriate for a while. However, when we continually find ourselves acting in ways that don't feel good or aren't moving us in a healthy direction, that's when we want to consider taking different actions.

Another phase I have found myself in is trying to acknowledge the fear. When we recognize the ways our past is invading our present, we can want to change, but damn it if that change doesn't terrify us. What if it doesn't work out? What if they don't give me what I need? What if I sound stupid? What if I lose all control? The worries are endless, and we can get spun out thinking about them all. The truth is, we don't know how it's going to work out, but we do know the ending if we keep doing the same thing.

It has been said that the definition of insanity is doing the same thing over and over and expecting different results. We need to recognize that it's scary and choose to do it anyway, which can feel like it goes against our better judgment. Remember, our nervous system is always looking for any threat, and doing something where the outcome is unknown feels like a credible threat. I think this is where we usually get stuck. We are uncomfortable, even unhappy with how things are, but we are also too scared to change.

THE WORST- AND BEST-CASE SCENARIOS PRACTICE

Whenever I find myself caught in this fear loop, I like to play out the different scenarios. If I don't, my anxious mind will spin out with all of the possible ways it could go wrong. I purposefully take my mind there first and consider the worst-case scenario. For me that was imagining myself opening up, asking for what I need, and the person I love looks me straight in the eyes and tells me that I am too much. That what I am asking for isn't something I am worthy of, or they tell me that someone else needs it more than I do, and I am selfish to even ask. Even writing this makes me want to curl up in a ball and cry. I know that starting with the worst scenario can seem counterintuitive. It would be logical to think that the best way to push back against fear would be to distract from it or at least ignore it. But when we do that, we only give it more power over us, so I like to jump right in, think it through, and give it my worst. Once I have considered the unfavorable outcome, it doesn't feel so scary anymore. I know it, have run myself through it, and can set it aside for a bit.

Next, I do the same thing for the best-case scenario. That would be having my requests met with attention, love, and support. Being heard, seen, and feeling important without having to do anything to earn it. It would also mean that the support I am receiving is consistent and becomes something I can count on without worrying about it. I can even ask those I am not incredibly close with to offer me some care, and when they do, it's magical and life-affirming. It's like a big breath in. I like to do the best-case scenario right after the worst-case because it pushes out those dark thoughts that could have come up while imagining it all going wrong.

Finally, I think about the most likely case, which is that communicating my needs will be uncomfortable, but when I select the right people to try it out on, it will be okay. I may fumble the first few tries, but since we already have a good relationship, they will stick around as I try again. I will also let them in on my process so that they understand what I am trying to do and hopefully support me along the way. No one is perfect, so I can't expect them to meet all of my needs, but they will do their best and I won't feel the urge to compete as strongly as I did before.

This practice, while time-consuming, helps me see things more clearly. You see, when I react out of fear, my amygdala (or what I like to call the fire alarm of our brain) sounds off and overrides my prefrontal cortex. This matters because the prefrontal cortex is responsible for decision-making, self-awareness, problem-solving, and much more.

For me to get to choose how I respond (a.k.a. change my behavior) I have to be calmer, and for that to happen I can't be working in the dark. Playing it out helps shed light on some of my fears, to figure out which ones are real and which are made up, and then I can relinquish some of that need for control and move in the right direction.

WE ARE WORTH SHOWING UP FOR

This feeling that we aren't enough as we are or that to be of value we have to prove it is more common than I thought. In October 2023 I shared in a video how I was struggling with burnout, and the number of comments stating "OMG me too!" blew my mind. I work a lot and go through phases of feeling overwhelmed, yet I know that regular breaks are important for self-care and long-term success. I asked myself in my morning journal, "Why is it so hard for me to take breaks?" and realized that I didn't think I had earned it. Then I asked myself, "What would it look like to earn a break?" and I didn't have an answer. I didn't know because it wasn't something I thought I could give myself. Someone else had to see it, tell me I was great, and show me how worthy I was. This was a shock, and went against my belief that I was independent and confident, when I so clearly felt that every kind word or loving touch had to be fought for or earned.

There was one phrase I used in the video that resonated with my community, and that was "hustling to prove that I am worth showing up for." The inconsistencies in our childhood can leave us believing that we aren't worth it or that we have to go the extra mile to get what should be readily given.

I know that I grew up feeling that way. My dad worked away from home a lot and I never really knew if he would be there for me. There were tons of times when he would say he'd make it to an important event only to be stuck in another state working. His presence was unpredictable and I spent most of my childhood striving for his attention. This caused me to believe that there was a scarcity of love or support and if I wanted something from someone else, I had to beat out others to get it. Otherwise, I would be left without.

MOVING TOWARD CHANGE

Spanish philosopher George Santayana once said, "Those who cannot remember the past are condemned to repeat it."[2] I would say that it's not really about remembering it. Everyone I have talked to remembers at least parts of what happened to them and the pain that they felt. It's more about understanding the past and its effect on us that stops us from repeating it.

Just like when I tried to stop competing with others by pretending I didn't care if I won. It didn't change how I felt or my urge to be the best, because I didn't yet understand the reason for my behavior. Once I knew that I was doing all that to get more love and attention, then I could do something about it. I could work on communicating my needs, ask for support, and express how upsetting inconsistency is to me. I could give those in my life a chance to meet my needs instead of trying to control them into happening. Which of course is easier said than done, but I did have a place to begin. I had to start talking about it.

Since I wasn't used to communicating about these things, I started by journaling out what I would say and imagining how people would respond. It was terrible, so I talked to my therapist about it, and she recommended I take these conversations slow so that people could digest what I was saying and have a chance to support me. Talk about terrifying. I was going to tell people what I needed from them in the hopes that they would just give it to me. I have never been more uncomfortable in my life. I started with my closest friend, sharing what I was working on in therapy and what I was trying to do. For some reason sharing my process made it easier to try this new communication thing out with her, and it also made her more understanding when I would struggle with it. Luckily, she got it, listened, and supported me. I am forever grateful to her, and it helped me argue back against that old belief that I had to consistently earn love and attention.

This type of growth and change takes time, and we will need to regularly do some internal research to keep it moving. Asking ourselves questions and being okay with the answers we find is key. I think that's the hardest, because sometimes what I learn about myself feels embarrassing and shameful, and I don't want to acknowledge it. But through recognition comes a greater awareness, and how can we change something we don't know is happening?

"WHY DO I KEEP DOING THIS?" EXERCISE— *QUESTIONS TO HELP CHANGE YOUR PERFECTIONIST WAYS*

1. If someone offers their support easily, are you able to accept it? Why or why not?
2. What behaviors do you think could be tied to your worth?
3. How often are you able to recognize and celebrate your wins? When are these wins linked to earning something?

4. When you encounter obstacles or setbacks, how do you typically respond?
5. Do you ever feel like you're in your own way? How often are you not taking advantage of opportunities because you don't think you deserve it?
6. If someone gives you an honest compliment, how do you react? Can you accept their kind words?

CONTROL CHALLENGE

For one task this week—whether it's an email, a workout, or a creative project—consciously aim for **good enough** instead of perfect. Set a reasonable time limit and stop when you reach it, resisting the urge to overedit or redo. Were you able to stop working when it was good enough? Reflect on how it felt to let go of perfection.

Chapter 3

PEOPLE-PLEASING, ANXIETY, AND MANIPULATION

Why We Can't Calm Down Until Everyone Is Happy

PUTTING OTHER PEOPLE FIRST IS SOMETHING WE ALL GREW UP learning about. As children, we're often forced to share our toys and told to play nicely with one another. We are encouraged to apologize to others if they appear upset, even when we haven't done anything wrong, and to agree with authority figures like teachers or other parents without question. Along the way we are praised if we are compliant, often called "easygoing" or "low-maintenance," reinforcing the idea that being agreeable and accommodating is more valuable than being assertive or authentic.

Many of these lessons instill values of generosity and cooperation, preparing us for collaborative environments later in life. Overall, there isn't anything wrong with doing this; we should teach our children to be respectful and kind to others. But we should also consider the limits to this type of interaction. While teaching our children to be kind and caring, we also want them to know when to stand up for themselves. We want them to know that there will be times when we give in and other times when we get our way. This ebb and flow of relationships and life should be discussed so that our children don't think they only have one option, to please others, and in turn carry that narrative through their adult lives.

If we are taught to always put others first, we risk neglecting our own needs and well-being. We may see ourselves as secondary citizens, our thoughts and preferences not being as important. This can have a detrimental effect on our confidence and shake our faith in ourselves. Instead of getting to know who we are and what we like, we can find ourselves looking out to others for those answers, feeling unsure of something until someone else tells us it's okay.

This can be even more apparent for those of us who grew up in tumultuous or abusive households. For example, having an alcoholic parent meant we were never sure which version of them we would encounter: the sad yet kind sober parent or the harmful and angry drunk one. We can start to believe from a young age that our emotional and physical safety depended on their mood, and therefore it was in our best interest to make sure they were always happy. Or at the very least, we didn't want to give them a reason to be upset with us.

Growing up in these types of environments where our focus is always outward on others can cause us to constantly put their emotional state above our own, ultimately leading to a need to control our emotions or actions. We can walk on eggshells trying not to say or do anything upsetting for fear of the ramifications. Without realizing it, we can feel that our safety depends on our ability to keep those around us happy. In psychology, we call this response "fawning," and it's one of the often-forgotten versions of our stress response and a root cause of our controlling behavior.

FAWNING

Our stress response is most often referred to as our fight-or-flight response. While those two options are the first line of defense against something threatening, we can't always run away or fight back. This leaves us with the less active responses of freeze and fawn. When we aren't strong enough to fight or fast enough to run away, we can play dead or freeze, hoping that our attacker will lose interest. Think of us ignoring the bullies at school wishing that they would just go away. We can even dissociate or remove ourselves a bit from our reality and go to our happy place for a bit until the situation has ended. However, for many of us, this isn't enough, so we resort to fawning.

At its core, fawning is about control, but in a way that looks like surrender. It means that we try our hardest, using all of our resources, and do everything in our power to try and please the person who has been hurting us. We think that if we keep them happy, they won't do the damaging thing anymore. This can apply to abusive relationships but also where there is an addiction present because we think it's up to us to keep them from drinking or doing drugs.

But how do you know if you're fawning?

- Do you constantly suppress your own needs to keep someone else comfortable?
- Do you feel responsible for managing someone else's emotions, even at your own expense?
- Do you agree to things you don't want to do just to avoid conflict?
- Do you struggle to say no because you're afraid of upsetting someone?

If you recognize yourself in these questions, you might be engaging in fawning—a trauma response rooted in survival.

Sometimes, we may fawn because we're afraid of conflict or rejection, believing that if we keep everything peaceful, we'll be safe from the pain of being abandoned or unloved. But in trying to control how others feel or act, we lose control over ourselves—our needs, our emotions, and our sense of self.

Fawning isn't just extreme people-pleasing—it's self-erasure in the name of safety. And the hardest part? It often doesn't even work. No matter how much we try to keep others happy, their reactions aren't actually in our control.

We can find ourselves acting in this way for many reasons, one of which is codependency. This is applicable because we can't talk about people-pleasing without acknowledging codependency's role in it. Codependency is defined as an "excessive emotional or psychological reliance on a partner, typically one who requires support on account of an illness or addiction." It is often the soil from which people-pleasing blooms. We usually hear of this behavior when talking about families where there's addiction, but that's not the only place it exists. Sometimes we struggle with codependency because we've learned from a young age that our worth is tied to how well we care for others, leading us to believe that if we're not needed, we're not valued. In short, when we are codependent, we control our needs by suppressing them to meet the needs of another.

This could be through us losing our sense of self in a new relationship, enabling someone else's destructive behavior, or even suppressing our emotions to not upset others. A good example of this is a story shared by a member of my community, Yvette:

> *For as long as I can remember, I've been the one who listens. The friend who always has a shoulder for you to cry on, the family member who can be counted on in a crisis, the colleague who is always willing to take on an extra task. People often tell me how strong and reliable I am, and I've carried that label with pride. But recently, I realized that my strength has come at a cost.*

I struggle with speaking up for myself. I am forty-eight years old and you would think that I could say what's on my mind, but I can't. And it's not that I can't say I like or don't like something, it's more that I always put other people's needs first because I believe that they are more important than mine. I rarely, if ever, express my own emotional needs, no matter how small.

This revelation has been both shocking and disheartening. I feel like I have been living a lie, pretending to be okay with everything, when in reality I am drowning in unspoken feelings and unmet needs. I am often passive-aggressive with those I love, and I think it's because I don't ever tell them what I want or how I feel. This makes me wonder if all of my relationships are built on this lie because I don't know if anyone really knows who I am. Do I even know who I am? I honestly don't know what to do, I feel so lost.

Yvette never felt okay to speak up or share what she needed because she believed that it was her duty to care for everyone else first. Her need to be needed by others got in the way of her being able to be herself and grow in her relationships. In trying to control her own desires to support others, she unintentionally stunted her personal growth. To use one of my favorite phrases, she lit herself on fire to keep others warm.

WITHOUT BOUNDARIES

Codependency isn't the only reason we can find ourselves fawning or people-pleasing. It could also be due to "enmeshment," a concept introduced by therapist Salvador Minuchin in 1974 to describe what happens when a relationship or an entire family doesn't have clear and firm boundaries.[1] This means that there isn't any separation between what is yours and what is mine, and that can go for emotions too. How you feel can easily become how I feel, and I can believe that I am equally responsible for your mood and experience. Furthermore, this type of closeness doesn't allow for healthy independence and is often referred to as "emotional incest."

Enmeshment is a tricky issue to call out in therapy because we often believe that this is what makes our family loving and close. We can take pride in it and even feel safer as a result, but closeness should not come at the cost of our independence. When we grow up in a home like this, it can be hard for us to learn how to regulate our own emotions or make decisions independently. We can feel like we don't know who we are if we aren't with our family, and we can even abandon our own goals to keep the family together. This can make us scared of the outside world, feel anxious when we aren't with our family, and do everything we can to keep the group together.

An example of this comes from Gabby, a member of my community. She shares:

> *I was always proud of my family and the fact that we had remained so active in each other's lives. Whenever anyone acted shocked at how often we talked or saw each other, I used to just tell them that we were close and always had been. Recently, my therapist has started to point out some of the ways that my family may be too close, and that that is due to a lack of healthy boundaries. It's been hard for me to accept because my parents just want us to feel loved and know that they are always there for us.*
>
> *But if I am honest, I do see some issues, like the fact that I wanted to go away for school, but my family didn't support it and told me they couldn't understand why I would want to be that far away from them. I felt so much shame for even considering a college in a neighboring state, and I still feel guilty about that today. They strongly encouraged all of us—I have two sisters—to get a job in town and live close by. All but one of us did just that, and*

my youngest sister, who moved away, is often called selfish and my parents say that she just doesn't understand what the word "family" means.

While there are still things I love about having a close family, I can't shake the fact that it's actually unhealthy the way it is. I can't make decisions without talking to my mom, and I would still like to travel outside of our area, see the world, and maybe even live somewhere else. But I feel trapped, because I don't want to lose them, and I know they wouldn't approve. It sucks feeling like I have to either keep doing what I am doing or lose my family.

Gabby's story sheds light on the complexities of close-knit families and the challenge of maintaining healthy boundaries in an environment where control is deeply woven into relationships. Her experience shows how enmeshment, often disguised as care or closeness, can blur boundaries and create feelings of guilt, shame, and limitation in personal growth. While she cherishes her family's support, Gabby is beginning to see how establishing boundaries is essential—not just for her independence, but for breaking free from the unspoken control that has kept her feeling trapped or judged as she pursues her own aspirations. This story highlights the critical balance needed in relationships: fostering closeness while respecting individual autonomy and the freedom to make choices that align with our personal goals and happiness.

Healthy boundaries don't separate us from our loved ones; instead, they allow us to love ourselves and them at the same time. Without them, we can struggle to figure out who we are, what we like, and explore all of our options. The expectations placed on us to share everything, be connected all the time, and always put the family first can impede our development. In some cases, it can even cause us to resent the family we used to treasure.

BEING A GOOD PERSON

When we talk about people-pleasing we often think that it's synonymous with being a Good Samaritan. That we consider other people's feelings first and do everything in our power to make them feel better. At least that's how I have always thought of it, and why I used to wear this trait like a badge of honor. In many ways, I thought this made me a good person, an amazing friend, and the best daughter. However, through my own therapeutic work, I realized that people-pleasing didn't have anything to do with other people; it was all about me.

I still remember the session clearly; I was talking with my therapist about how resentful I had become of a good friend of mine. I had recently helped her move, driven to her house for our last four hangouts, and was always the one to call and check in on her. The relationship was starting to wear on me. I was telling my therapist how frustrated I was that I was always expected to be the one who gave, and she was the one who took. My therapist stopped me midsentence and asked how we decided where we would meet when we got together. I had to think about it because it didn't feel like we decided together, and then it hit me—I would just offer. I would always say it was no big deal, that I could just drive her way, no problem. Then she asked how my friend responded when I didn't offer, and the truth was, that never happened.

My therapist let me sit with this revelation for a minute and then asked me about the other issues I had brought up, and it hit me like a ton of bricks. I was the one who did these things unprompted. I was the one controlling the dynamic. I gave extra energy to the relationship without being asked, and then was upset when I did it. It's as if I tied myself up and then wanted to whine about how restricting the ropes I chose were. It was shocking and is still one of the most intense revelations I have ever had in therapy. But why on earth would I do this to myself? And how do I stop ruining my relationships and myself?

To answer those questions, I had to figure out what I got out of it and how I benefited from my behavior. This part of therapy isn't always easy, and this took me weeks to figure out. I first considered that it could have to do with my caretaking nature. I was always considered the most mothering in my friend group, so maybe that's where this was coming from. My therapist assured me that that wasn't it.

Next, I believed that it was because I truly enjoyed seeing other people happier. She assured me that we were getting closer, but that was still not the full truth. It wasn't until a different friend of mine offered to come my way for dinner the following week that I was faced with the real reason: It made me anxious to have other people do nice things for me.

We have discussed the fact that my worth is rooted in my ability to be helpful and of service to others. So what happens when someone doesn't allow me to do things for them? The truth is, I become incredibly uncomfortable. When I can't help, it feels like I'm not fulfilling my role or "earning my keep," as if my value is directly tied to what I can do for others. This triggers a deep sense of anxiety because I start to question my place in the relationship. I worry that if I'm not actively contributing or putting them first, they might think less of me or even be upset with me.

To cope with this anxiety, I immediately try to control the situation by finding ways to do something nice for them, almost as if I owe them for any kindness they've shown me. It's not really about their needs; it's about calming my own discomfort and ensuring the stability of our relationship. As my therapist pointed out, "People-pleasing behavior is simply another form of manipulation. You do everything you can to try and make them happy so that you can feel okay." Even though it was hard to hear at first, I realized she was right. I couldn't tolerate the idea of someone being upset, so I did everything in my power to make sure they were happy, not necessarily for their sake, but to ease my own anxiety.

OVERCORRECTION

We can't control other people. If they want to be upset they will be, and if they won't accept our help we can't force it upon them. While I think we can all agree that that's true, we still act in the hope that we can affect someone else's experience. This is why people-pleasing is such a common form of control and hard to shake. We know that without healthy boundaries in place and checking in with ourselves, other people can affect our day or how we feel. Therefore, we assume we have the same influence on others in the other direction. And that's not entirely wrong. We may impact how others are feeling by our actions, but that doesn't mean we can control how they manage their emotions or reactions. It also doesn't make us responsible for putting their experience ahead of our own. For many of us, it's difficult to find a good way of considering others without losing touch with ourselves.

A great example of this struggle comes from Amy, a member of my community and fellow recovering people-pleaser:

> *I've always been the type of person who puts others first. Growing up in a large family, I learned early on the importance of taking care of those around me. Whether it was helping my younger siblings with their homework or staying up late to lend a listening ear to a friend, I found joy and purpose in being there for others. But as I navigated my twenties and early thirties, I began to realize that my selflessness was taking a toll on me.*
>
> *It started subtly. I would skip meals to finish a project for work or cancel plans with friends because a colleague needed my help.*

I justified it by telling myself that I was being a good person and that my value was in my ability to support others. But over time, these small sacrifices accumulated, and I found myself feeling exhausted, burnt out, and resentful.

One day, I hit a breaking point. I had been working late every night for weeks, trying to meet an impossible deadline. My body ached, my mind was foggy, and I felt like I was on the verge of tears all the time. I confided in a friend, who gently suggested that maybe it was time to start putting myself first.

At first, the idea seemed selfish and foreign. How could I prioritize my needs when there were so many people depending on me? But I was desperate for change, so I decided to give it a try. I began setting boundaries at work, saying no to extra projects, and carving out time for activities that brought me joy. I started meditating, going for long walks, and reconnecting with hobbies I had long abandoned.

Initially, it felt liberating. I finally had time to breathe, to think, to be. But as the weeks went by, I noticed another shift. I became so focused on self-care that I began to neglect the people around me. I missed my sister's birthday because I was at a yoga retreat. I didn't call my mom back for days because I was "taking a break from screens." I let the pendulum swing too far in the opposite direction, and now I find myself feeling guilty and disconnected.

When we realize that our urge to put others first is getting in the way of our own lives, we can want to drastically change the way we interact, but that isn't always the solution. In Amy's case, she let the pendulum swing too far the other way and ended up feeling detached and remorseful. Instead of making a big change, it's better to start small. Consider the small actions we could take that would have some impact.

For example, when I was trying to change my people-pleasing behavior, I began by trying to not overapologize. It sounds small and simple, but it was (and still is) incredibly hard for me to do.

OVERAPOLOGIZING

To give you an idea of just how much I overapologize, let me take you back to my middle school softball tournament. I am left-handed and was working on doing a drag bunt, which just means that you run as you try to bunt the ball. It's hard, and you don't have much time to make it work. My coach was giving me pointers on ways to ensure I didn't pop the ball up and get out. As he was walking me through all the things I was doing that could be a bit better, I kept apologizing. "You should make sure you don't tilt the bat at too much of an angle." "Sorry," I would say. "Remember to keep your head down as you move." "I am so sorry, I will do better next time." Our conversation went on like this, until finally, he snapped back at me. He told me that I didn't need to apologize for every little thing, I just needed to listen and try to do better next time. I remember him saying, "Just stop apologizing so much, Kati!" as I ran out into center field for the next inning. What did I do? I turned back and said, "Sorry, I will try and stop."

This type of behavior went on for years until my therapist in college brought it up. She said she had noticed that I apologized a lot and asked if I was aware I was doing it. The truth was, I wasn't. Other than the one scenario with my coach, no one else had mentioned it. Since she thought it was worth exploring, she gave me homework. I had to try and keep track of how many times I said "sorry" over the next week and bring that back into our next session. The number was high, and within the first day I knew I had a problem. I didn't even keep an accurate count. I just remember going into my next session and telling her it was bad, and I was embarrassed.

She didn't push me for an actual number. She just asked that I keep being aware of how often I say it and try not to apologize when I couldn't identify what it was I was sorry for.

You know what I learned? That I say "sorry" an awful lot for someone who isn't sorry about much. I could come up with only a few examples of when I felt that I was sorry. It often had to do with me being in someone's way or bumping into them in public. Other than that, I was just saying it. It didn't mean what it was supposed to. All of my apologies had nothing to do with guilt or remorse, and more to do with me trying to keep other people happy. To prove that I was a good and kind person and that I respected those around me. Of course, I wanted to know what I could do to stop this. How could I learn to not say "sorry" all the time and not feel like a jerk as a result?

I realized that people-pleasing was a form of self-abandonment. When all my energy and focus went into pleasing others, I neglected myself, which weakened my connection to my own needs and emotions.

RECONNECTING WITH OURSELVES

Since people-pleasing is really about us trying to control other people and make them happy so that we can feel okay, we are going to have to put up some boundaries between ourselves and others. There needs to be some separation between how we feel and how other people feel. Sounds simple enough, but I can tell you that placing and upholding boundaries can be a minefield.

When I first started trying to set boundaries, I immediately felt like I was being mean or disrespectful. If I was in someone's way and didn't apologize for it, that made me the bad guy. Not being able to show just how kind and caring I was started to wear on me. It made me question my worth and who I was. I have always thought of myself as a caretaker, the one who goes the extra mile, a great friend, and someone you can always count on. Not consistently putting others first made me think that those things couldn't be true anymore. I felt like I was losing myself.

My therapist assured me that this was all part of the process and that by making this change I would finally get to know myself and who I was without the input of others. This is what makes boundary setting so tricky. We can base our entire sense of self on what we can give to others. Challenging that can be scary. I also think it can feel overwhelming because placing boundaries sounds like I am putting up walls to keep people out. Instead, boundaries are simply the parameters around a relationship that allow for us to simultaneously love ourselves and someone else. This process also helped me to realize that boundaries aren't about confrontation or me telling other people what's okay and not okay. It's about what I am going to do to take care of myself.

For example, a boundary isn't me saying, "You can't talk to me that way anymore." A boundary is about what I am going to do. Meaning that if someone is talking poorly to us, we can leave, hang up, or not talk to them as often. Sure, it's helpful for us to communicate about this up front, but that's not always necessary or helpful. Sometimes the silence or boundary itself can be enough. Let's say our sister constantly texts us hurtful things and puts us down. We don't have to reply or even acknowledge that we received those texts. The silence itself is the boundary. If she later texts us a question about something unrelated, we can reply to that.

I DON'T WANT TO FIGHT

As someone who is very conflict averse, I struggle with telling people that I can't do something or that I don't like the way they are speaking to me. I much prefer the silent boundary option, but I know that that's not always what's best for my relationships. We can't expect people to just read our minds and understand, and not giving them a chance to change or apologize can be damaging. Here's a recent comment I received about just that:

> "*I struggle so much with boundary setting! I tried to just not reply to my mom when she would say mean things, but then she calls me and I have to ignore her. It's like the pressure keeps building and then she has my other sister reach out to see if I am okay. I feel like my lack of communication is causing me more upset than if I just told her what I didn't like. But I am afraid that if I do we will get into a fight, and I just can't deal with any more arguments. They don't get us anywhere and I always end up apologizing in the end.*

This is why it's helpful for us to consider how we would communicate with our loved ones about our boundaries. In my experience, it's easier to make it all about myself by stating that I am working on myself and therefore will be trying to be more kind and thoughtful about the way I interact with them. When things stray away from that, I can refer back to that conversation. Saying something like, "Remember last week when I told you I was trying to be more kind and thoughtful? It feels like this conversation isn't going in that direction. Let's take a break and reconnect in a bit." Sure, people can get upset, angry even, but again, we can't control that. We can only control what we do, and as long as we are communicative and consistent, it will get easier. Change is always uncomfortable at first, and it can take some time for both sides to get the hang of it, but keep in mind that this will improve the relationship.

The next boundary-setting hurdle I had to overcome was saying no when I needed to. I had this nasty habit of always saying yes to things even if I didn't have the time or energy to do them. Then I would be rushing around, stressed out, and often resentful of the thing I was doing. Even though it sounded terrible to me, my therapist assured me that saying no when I wasn't able to do something was completely fine and healthy.

While I thought this form of boundary setting would be more difficult because of the communication involved, it wasn't. If someone invited me out to a party, but I had previously told another friend that I would meet them earlier that day for lunch, I could just say that I already had plans. If someone asked for my help moving, getting things ready for their big trip, or even with their kid's birthday party, I had the right to say no. While the guilt would come, and at first I would end up giving in anyway, it did get easier.

The most incredible part of this work was that when I said no to the things I didn't want to do, it left more room for the things I did enjoy, and I found myself having a good time more often! It sounds obvious, but I didn't realize how many things I was doing out of obligation, not actual desire, and this shift made my life more enjoyable.

GRIEVING THE LOSS

The hardest part about this whole process is always the unpredictable way people will react. It's a reminder that control really is at the root of the behaviors we want and need to change. Whenever I am trying to communicate a healthy boundary to someone in my life and they lash out or play the victim, that tells me that the boundary was desperately needed. I was just giving in to everything they wanted. When someone responds well and respects it, well, it's likely that that relationship wasn't really off track. While the people-pleaser in me wishes that everyone would hear me out, understand, and support these new ways of interacting, that's not reality. Doing this work has shown me that I was in some great relationships that were balanced and loving, and I was also in some very selfish ones that didn't work if I wasn't doing everything they wanted.

The grief that I felt when some of what I considered my closest relationships ended was heavy. It was also sad that they were all predicated on me giving more than my share in most scenarios. I still remember continually checking my phone to see if one of my friends had texted me back, each time feeling more disappointed and like a loser. I had recently tried talking to her about how our relationship felt one-sided. I wasn't ever able to reach her when I needed anything, yet she would get mad if I wasn't available 24/7 to her. I told her that didn't feel fair, and that I would like for us to have a more balanced relationship. She acted fine but then went right back into her old ways after about a week.

When I reached out to her seeking insight and support, she never responded. About a week later, she called me in a panic, asking to meet because she had caught her boyfriend in a lie. I wasn't in town, and when I explained that I wasn't available, she responded passive-aggressively, saying, "Well, I guess you don't really care about me." It became clear to me that I needed to create some distance, and eventually the relationship faded away. It would be easy to say that these endings are healthy and good and we should be proud of ourselves, but it's hard and lonely at first. It takes time to process the loss before being able to see it in a positive light. I still feel the pain of these lost relationships, but it has lessened as I worked through it. Not to mention that it has opened me up to new, more balanced friendships, and that feels good.

BOUNDARIES I HAVE WITH MYSELF

Throughout this process, I also learned that there are different types of boundaries depending on the relationship and dynamic. For example, if someone I don't know tries to hold my hand, I am going to pull it away and not allow that physical contact. That's one of my physical boundaries. There are also boundaries we have in our sex lives, what we are okay sharing emotionally or not, and how we feel about sharing our material goods with others. There are many types of boundaries in our lives, but the ones I have the toughest time with are my internal boundaries. These are things like keeping the promises I make to myself, making time for my goals, and talking to myself in a kind and loving way. When I am not keeping these boundaries, it's harder for me to uphold the others.

I recently did *The Artist's Way* workbook with a friend, and one of the weekly assignments was to go on an artist date. This had to be something we enjoyed doing, that was fulfilling in some way, and we had to do it alone. It didn't have to be a big deal or cost a lot of money. It could be something like going to sit at your favorite coffee shop or walking through a local museum. Each week I would promise myself that I would make time for something nice, something I love doing, and each week I let myself down. In the twelve weeks that we moved through that workbook, I went on exactly two artist dates. It was shameful, but even more of a reminder that I struggle to put myself first. I would tell myself that it was selfish, that my husband would want to come, that I really should be doing something else, or that I just didn't have time this week. As the weeks passed, I became so angry with myself. Why couldn't I do this simple thing? Why was it so hard for me to take a minute to myself?

I realized that it was because it felt wrong to do something only because I wanted to. It seemed self-indulgent and unnecessary to put energy into such a self-serving task. I believed that my worth was contingent upon my ability to put others first, always. These artist dates were forcing me to do the opposite, and it didn't feel right. It was highlighting a piece of my people-pleasing behavior that I hadn't noticed yet, and like any important change, it was terrifying and uncomfortable at first. However, if I can push through, try it anyway, and sit in that discomfort, maybe I can feel more energized and fulfilled, and begin to create from a place of abundance rather than depletion.

Our internal boundaries are the foundation on which the others are built. This is why I am continually trying to do better, being aware of the importance of the things I want and making sure I create time for them. It's hard to put myself first—I feel guilty and selfish—but I know that I can't show up for other people if I don't first show up for myself. In that way, I use my people-pleasing urge to my advantage. The thought that I can't help others without helping myself is just the catch I need to keep working on myself. It helps me fight harder to uphold my internal boundaries, trying to do better, and be better, for myself and everyone around me.

"WHY DO I KEEP DOING THIS?" EXERCISE—*QUESTIONS TO IDENTIFY AND CHANGE YOUR PEOPLE-PLEASING URGES*

1. In what situations do you find it most challenging to share what you prefer or identify what you want to do?
2. How often do you find yourself apologizing?
3. When you agree to do things for others, how often do you feel resentful or regret saying yes?
4. How often do you feel like you are prioritizing your wants and needs? What can you do to further identify your wants/needs and prioritize them more often?
5. What is something you love doing? How often do you make time to do it?
6. What are some of your internal boundaries? How often do you uphold them?

CONTROL CHALLENGE

Before agreeing to any request, practice pausing. Instead of immediately saying yes, respond with:

- "Let me check my schedule and get back to you."
- "I need a moment to think about it."

This gives you time to assess whether you genuinely want to say yes or if you're only agreeing out of obligation.

Chapter 4

TAKING UP SPACE AND FEELING LIKE TOO MUCH

Why We Shrink Ourselves to Gain Connection

THE IDEA OF TAKING UP SPACE CAN BE DIFFICULT TO GRASP because it goes beyond the physical—our bodies, belongings, and presence. It also includes the emotional and psychological space we occupy in the world and in the lives of others. This can mean expressing our needs, sharing our ideas, allowing ourselves to play, or advocating for ourselves.

Unlike physical space, which has clear boundaries, this kind of space is subjective and harder to define. Because there are no set rules, it's easy to feel uncertain about how much space we're allowed to take. We might fear overstepping or feel guilty for asserting ourselves. This is where control comes in—without clear limits, we may try to manage or minimize our presence to avoid discomfort. We may hold back, shrink ourselves, or hesitate to take up space at all, unsure of what is "too much." The lack of defined boundaries can make it challenging to trust that we belong.

Some of us can easily carve out our territory and share our emotional responses as needed, but many of us aren't so sure. We can think that other people have more of a right to it, that we are being greedy, or that our existence is already taking up too much space.

The feeling of being too much is contingent upon there being a correct amount of space that each of us should take up. However, that amount doesn't exist, and this feeling that we are somehow too large, too loud, or too emotional for our lives can ultimately limit and control how much we do.

The easy answer here would be to say that we should all stop shrinking ourselves, take up the space we need, and be who we are. However, those actions can feel like they come with some stiff consequences, and the potential cost often outweighs any benefit. It can be safer to stay small, not make a sound, and hold on to the relationships we have, to maintain the connections in our lives that are important to us.

The interesting thing about being "too much" is that no one knows exactly what it means, but they can tell you what it feels like. It's not something we can measure or define; it has to be felt to be understood. The experience itself is subjective and what might feel like too much to one person may not be experienced that way by another. Just as one person may describe the emotion of joy as passionate and exhilarating while another might perceive it as overwhelming and erratic.

WHERE DOES THIS FEELING COME FROM?

In many ways, our perception of what is enough and what is too much begins with the parameters set by our parents, and is often done without conscious thought. This can mean that these boundaries have been passed down from generation to generation. They have more to do with where our parents were in their lives or what experiences they grew up with rather than with what we needed. Either way, they aren't often created with us in mind, and can leave us feeling like we just don't fit.

Imagine yourself as a child, around eight or nine years old. Whenever you want to goof around or show your parents something fun you've just learned, they tell you, "Not now," or, worse, shout at you to stop bothering them. This pattern continues as you grow up, and over time you begin to believe it's not okay to express yourself or show others who you are.

As these experiences accumulate, you might start to receive compliments from others about how well-behaved, respectful, and ideal you are as a child. This reinforces the notion that hiding your true self is better and safer. Gradually, this can shape your beliefs about yourself, leading you to think that you're not important enough or are an inconvenience.

When encouraged to speak up or share your thoughts, you might choose to control your voice and stay silent, not wanting to upset anyone or feeling that others have more valuable things to say. If this resonates with you, you might often feel like you're too much—an ever-present sensation that follows you everywhere. Like this story I received from a member of my community:

> "*I remember from a very young age, maybe six or seven, always living "in my head." Recently I've begun to understand that it was because growing up when I showed big emotions I was told I was "dramatic," "oversensitive," and "getting carried away." So I tended to keep everything inside. Shove it down. Ironically people then pegged me as "shy," or "introverted," or slow to warm up. This became very confusing for a little girl and I became unable to know how I was supposed to deal with intense situations. I felt like something was wrong with me. And now in my forties, I'm only beginning to process so many feelings and little-t traumas. And it's HARD, and at times painful. And I have a long way to go. Because feeling like there was something broken about me and*

trying to not be noticed led to self-harm and eating disorders to cope with the massive amount of repressed feelings.

The way we were talked to and engaged with in our developmental years helps us form our sense of self and, in a way, figure out how much space we think we should take up. If we were given free rein to express ourselves, then it's likely that we feel we can be assertive and independent without shame or fear. When we feel angry we know we can show it, and when we are sad we can lean on our parents for support and understanding. Without this freedom we quickly learn that to stay safe we have to pretend that many parts of who we are don't exist, contorting ourselves to fit within the given parameters. We believe we have to shrink ourselves to sustain the only connections we have.

As children, we have limited resources and often cling to anything that gives us a sense of control or stability—patterns that inevitably follow us into adulthood. The one thing we have full autonomy over is ourselves. So when we feel like we don't fit in or are taking up too much space, we don't question the rules or who created them; instead, we try to change and control ourselves. It can feel like our only option.

Another crucial aspect of this is recognizing that our urge to shrink ourselves didn't come out of nowhere; it seemed like a good idea for a reason. Some experiences caused us to believe that the way we were wasn't correct, prompting us to seek the opposite. If we were loud, we thought we needed to be quiet. If we needed connection, we thought we should be more independent. This experience can come from many places, but there are common themes I've seen and experienced over the years.

The first, most common role in feeling like you and your emotions are too much is empathy. If we feel intensely for others and express these concerns, we might be told that we are too sensitive.

As someone who knows they're more sensitive than most, I'm often told that I worry too much about how others feel and that I need to relax or ignore others' experiences. But no matter how hard I try, I can't. When I see someone in pain, it's almost as if it's happening to me, and I can't just look the other way.

Realizing that most people don't think about others as much or aren't as pained by watching someone get their feelings hurt has made me hesitant to speak up over the course of my life. I already know that if I say something, I'll be told that I'm too sensitive or too dramatic, so I preemptively acknowledge those things about myself and stuff that feeling down. It feels like my emotions aren't appropriate, so why give someone the chance to remind me of that?

The next common role is "parentification." This can happen if one or both of our parents depend on us for their emotional support rather than filling their role as our primary caregivers. This can mean that they turn to you for understanding and counseling as they navigate a tricky situation, or even expect you to pick up other parental roles that they can't complete. We could find ourselves taking on the primary role of caring for our younger siblings, being solely responsible for packing their lunches and getting them up for school. Instead of getting to be a child and develop at a regular pace, we took on a higher level of responsibility at a young age, skipping ahead to a parental role. This experience is often referred to as being "parentified" as a child. When we are parentified children we can feel overly responsible from a young age and begin to believe that we aren't loved for who we are, but instead for what we can do for others. We may have been taught that the needs of those around us are important, that we're responsible for meeting those needs, and that our needs are less important or should take up less space.

Feeling like too much could also be due to trauma. I know it can seem like we blame a lot of things on trauma, but that's because it is deeply wounding and can shake us to our core. It also can result from smaller traumas compiling over the years to have an impact on our development and experiences. These are often referred to as the "little-t traumas" mentioned in the example above.

When something happens to us that makes us fear for our own life or safety, we don't trust ourselves or our world. When we are harmed by someone who was supposed to love and care for us, it has an even greater effect. As a way of preventing future harm, we can become acutely aware of people's moods and facial expressions, using this information to try our best not to rock the boat. In many ways, we can want to disappear, as if our being here is the problem.

This is why we can feel like we are walking on eggshells, trying to do everything perfectly so that we don't upset someone. We can worry that if we do speak up about any of our wants or needs, we will be told to sit down and shut up. We can feel like it's not safe to be ourselves or to have any thoughts or opinions, slowly starting to believe that we are simply too much.

One form of trauma that can have a large impact on this experience is neglect. We often think of trauma as something that is done to us, but it can also occur because of things that weren't done for us. If we grew up in a home where our needs and concerns were overlooked or ignored, we can start to think that our needs aren't real or even worth having. Many of my patients have told me that they just thought they were overreacting and that most children didn't need all of the attention they craved. That something must be wrong with them.

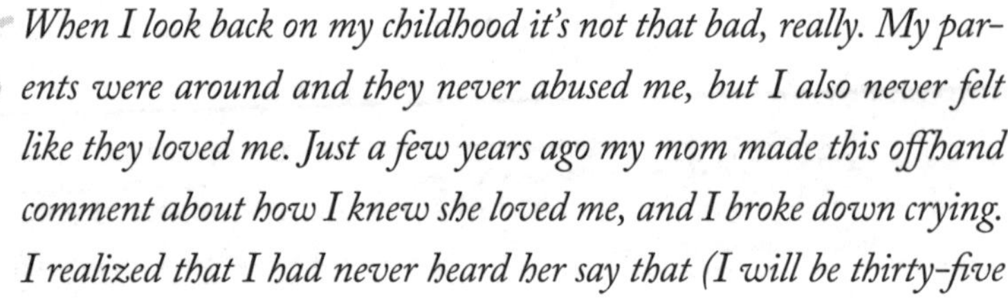

When I look back on my childhood it's not that bad, really. My parents were around and they never abused me, but I also never felt like they loved me. Just a few years ago my mom made this offhand comment about how I knew she loved me, and I broke down crying. I realized that I had never heard her say that (I will be thirty-five

next month) and I always thought I was the problem, that I was too needy or the amount of attention I craved wasn't reasonable.

WANTING TO DISAPPEAR

When we have been raised to believe that we are too much, we exert control by trying to be smaller, less intrusive, and shrink ourselves so we're not in the way, many times manifesting in disordered eating. As an eating disorder specialist, I have seen this particular feeling play out with many of my patients, just like this story from Ellie:

> "*For as long as I can remember, I have thought that I was too much. One of my earliest memories was of my father telling me to stop crying and being angry that I was always upset. He also loved to say that children were supposed to be seen and not heard any time me or my sister bothered him. So as soon as I could, I learned not to feel anything and to stuff any emotion I had down deep so that it wouldn't upset my dad. Even though he's dead now, I still worry that I am going to upset him.*
>
> *It felt like if I was being myself I was going to make somebody mad. All I have ever wanted to do was disappear, and I remember restricting what I ate and loving that I kept getting smaller. I actually believed that my dad would love me more if I was just less inconvenient, which is so sad for me to say now. At the time I thought that not eating gave me some control over the situation and that by getting to a certain size I could prove that I wasn't too much. However, at the age of forty-eight, I realize that I still think I am taking up too much space and there isn't any amount of weight I can lose that will change that belief. Honestly, I don't know what else to do to help, though, because I still feel like I am the problem.*

When we have this deeply held belief that what we want and need is too much, we can control what we give our body by restricting what we eat or simply ignoring it. We pretend we aren't hungry and don't need to buy food, thinking that if we shrink ourselves down we will be more accepted or at least not take up as much space. The thing about eating disorders, though, is that it's not really about the food. It's about the urge to shrink ourselves away so we feel safer. We believe that the less space we take up, physically and emotionally, the better we'll feel and the more people will like us. That the love we all deserve is somehow contingent upon us not having any needs or taking any space from someone else. We can believe that to exist and be safe we have to disappear.

Unfortunately, feeling like we want to disappear is common. We think we're just in the way, can never do things right, and that others would be better off without us. So we remove ourselves from situations, relationships, and specific roles in our lives, believing this will shield others from our issues, simplify their lives, or make them happier. However, this is rarely, if ever, the case. Withdrawing and isolating doesn't protect anyone; it hurts everyone involved.

When we focus on disappearing or shrinking ourselves, we aren't able to see any solutions. We concentrate solely on making ourselves smaller, even though it doesn't make us feel better. Instead, it's helpful to examine the parameters placed upon us, understand where these limits came from, and explore how they can be adjusted. Rather than trying to take up less space, we need to figure out how to make room for ourselves, recognizing our right to exist fully and authentically.

PARTS WORK

Sometimes the urge to shrink ourselves doesn't come from a need to disappear completely, but rather that we can only show pieces of ourselves that we deem acceptable. As if there are parts of who we are that we should ignore, or that seem like they need to be hidden in the back room so that the company doesn't know they are here. We could feel the urge to hide them away because of what others have said, or because of what we fear they might say. So we do just that. We stuff away certain parts of ourselves to control how we are perceived by others. This selective presentation is a defense mechanism, born from past experiences where vulnerability led to judgment or rejection. Consequently, we curate our identity, displaying only the aspects that we believe will be met with approval, to protect ourselves from potential harm.

I recently moved to a new part of the country and thus had to find a new therapist. In an effort to challenge myself past where I have worked so far, I found a therapist who practiced styles of therapy I haven't practiced myself. After searching for the right fit, I found someone who practiced Internal Family Systems (IFS) as well as some other helpful therapeutic modalities. The interesting thing about IFS is that it focuses a lot of its work on the internal conflicts we have between the varying parts of ourselves, and this portion of therapy is called "parts work."

I had never participated in parts work before, but quickly learned that it didn't have to do with me feeling like I had different personalities within me, but that I had various pieces of myself that were responsible for contrasting parts of my personality. In my case, this meant that I had five distinct parts of my psyche that were in charge of my sense of self. Allowing each of these parts to show up, be heard, and reveal its purpose helped me understand where I had been shrinking or hiding myself in an attempt to control my environment and experiences.

The first step to identifying these parts and summoning them was to create a meeting place so they could arrive. I had to close my eyes and imagine what kind of place would feel good for me. What would be comfortable and safe enough for me to allow all of the thoughts and voices out, let them be seen and heard? As it turns out, this place was a local café with marble-topped tables and little wooden chairs. It was warm, friendly, and comfortable.

Next, we wait to see who shows up.

The first part to get there was the adult part of my psyche who is always in charge and is extraordinarily responsible, hence her early arrival. She is exhausted and overwhelmed, yet firmly believes that no one else can do her job. Therefore, she has tied herself to the very to-do list that she resents and is very unhappy about. Sadly, I hear from her the most. She is the part of me that is usually the loudest because she's the one in charge. She makes sure I get everything finished; in fact, she is the one ensuring that I write this book on time, while continuing to complete all of my other tasks. In many ways, I am grateful for her and would not be where I am without her. In IFS this type of part is called a "manager" because it's the part that I show to the world most often and it protects my other, more fragile or painful parts from being exposed to the world. The adult me is presentable and reliable, and who I draw most of my sense of self from.

Next to show up was my competitive part. She was a surprise, and for weeks I couldn't figure out why she was there or what her role was. Turns out a big part of me is constantly comparing myself to others, wanting to do better, be better, and gain recognition for my hard work. She works alongside my adult self, ensuring I stay focused, on task, and pushing forward. She can be relentless, but she's also the driving force behind much of my success in school and childhood. She's the reason I got straight As and made the varsity team. I can't deny she's a big part of who I am today. I've just had to learn how to better engage with her, so she doesn't push too hard and damage my relationships.

Then my party part decided to show up. She loves a good time and wouldn't want to miss out on an opportunity to see everyone. She is fun, excited, and doesn't worry about anything other than making memories and enjoying herself. She was most active when I was in college and throughout my twenties. As I have gotten older, she has faded a bit, but she is still a vital part of who I am and reminds me of the importance of having a good time in life. Since this part loves distractions, she is what IFS calls a "firefighter part" because her role is to divert attention away from anything painful. I always wish I could spend more time letting her run the show, but because I have adult responsibilities, she seems to get pushed to the side a lot and ignored.

Another part that showed up in my café was younger Kati; she is about eight years old and is the peacekeeper. She didn't want anyone fighting or getting upset, and is there to ensure everyone gets along. As a child, I never liked it when people argued or raised their voices. I have come to realize that it was because we never did that in my home. It's not that we all got along, but it just wasn't okay to fight about it. Instead, we went to our rooms or outside to walk it off. I never got to see someone fight, talk about it, and make up. I didn't know how anger or upset could be dealt with healthily. This is why this part showed up. She isn't comfortable with any arguments and was there to make sure they didn't happen. She would also be considered a firefighter part because her role is to stop anything painful from coming to the surface.

The final part to show up was the one that I didn't want to hear from or even see. In parts work we call these pieces of ourselves "exiled parts." These are the parts that are in pain; they are the ones that are expressing the upset for our entire system and dictating how our control manifests. In my case, this was teenage me. I think the reason this part showed up as a teenager was because it was a very emotional time in my life. Her role is to demand that I feel everything I wanted to ignore. I used to tell my therapist that she was my emotional Sherpa, laboring under all of the anger and sadness I didn't feel safe to express. She is so angry, crying all the time, and picking fights with the other parts, demanding to know why she is the one that has to stay silent. There were many sessions when she wouldn't even participate because she wasn't listened to. I didn't always want to dip into that emotional well, unsure of whether or not I could pull myself out when my therapy session ended.

I know this may all sound unusual, but this was by far the most healing work I have ever done in therapy. To imagine these different parts of myself as actual people and hear directly from them what they are thinking and feeling was powerful. I couldn't get away with just talking about my current stressors; I was forced to consider what was going on with each of these parts, and that in turn helped me see that there were huge chunks of myself that I didn't believe should exist. Parts of myself I didn't think were appropriate or acceptable.

From my perspective, the teenage part of me was too emotional, unpredictable, and embarrassing. Without much thought, I can easily see that somewhere deep within my belief system I agreed that I was too much and had to control these parts of myself. That my emotional expression shouldn't be shown to the world, that it wasn't allowable and should be hidden. The goal of IFS is to help us detangle ourselves from our various parts and get better connected with "the self" or the harmonious collection of all our parts. Along the way it also gave me a huge revelation as to why I felt so disconnected and angry. It helped me see that I was shrinking myself, keeping pieces of my true self hidden not only from those around me but also from myself. To feel better and more connected, I was going to have to listen to what my teen part had to say, embrace those emotions, and integrate them into my overall sense of self.

That's easier said than done, but the reason parts work is important here is because we may not even realize that we are hiding our true selves away or shrinking ourselves to fit into a specific situation. Taking stock of our parts can be eye-opening, and in my case it helped me see where I could work to change, and where I needed to make space.

FINDING THE SPACE WE NEED

When animals that have been in captivity are moved to the wild, it's common for them to freeze up, overwhelmed by the newfound freedom. They often don't know what to do with the extra space and show clear signs of stress. Many will huddle together, clinging to the familiar, and sometimes they refuse to venture out into their new environment. This reaction highlights the profound impact of captivity on their behavior and the challenges they face in adjusting to a more natural, expansive habitat.

It can take years for zoos to find the right place to release an animal, wanting to ensure that they have a group they can connect with and the right resources nearby. While I know we have evolved past our animal friends, we too can struggle to find the space we need, and even when we do, we may be scared to explore it.

The reason it can be so difficult for us to break out of these old parameters is because these boundaries feel safe. We know what to expect, and without them, we can feel like an animal let out of a cage for the first time, scared and unsure. We can worry that if we are our true selves no one will like us, and we will be more alone than ever. But before we even discuss being ourselves and our concerns about it not going well, we need to address the biggest issue I see in our path to taking up space—figuring out who we are.

I receive questions about this constantly, from people wondering how to figure out what they like, what they don't like, and what they want out of life. One I received this week reads:

> *How do you know "who you are" or have a sense of self if your childhood and adolescence were filled with multiple traumas and as a result, the only constant in your adulthood is the side effects of the trauma? How do you become a person once you are already an adult?*

It can be hard to find a road map to something that everyone else seems to have figured out without much effort. We can think that we should just know because we aren't children and have lived a long life, but I don't think of it this way. I have always believed that we are ever-evolving, figuring out new facets of ourselves, and trying to see the lines between those we are in relationships with and us, recognizing when we agree and disagree with someone. Every situation in our life has the opportunity to teach us something new about ourselves, so I would argue that our sense of self isn't fixed, but malleable and ever-changing. Instead of feeling like we are behind in figuring this out, we can see this as a great opportunity to join everyone else in their path to self-discovery.

If we have spent most of our lives trying to take up as little emotional space as possible, it's going to be difficult for us to shift away from that. We can find those old patterns of stuffing down how we feel and wanting to go with the flow tugging on us, telling us they are easier and more comfortable. Which is why the first step is to do some things on our own. This isn't because we are isolating, but because we are trying to get to know ourselves, and the best way to get to know someone is to spend some time with them.

GETTING TO KNOW YOU

As I confessed earlier, I suck at doing things on my own, so I know this first task is a big one, and it's okay to start with little bits of time. I find things that take less than an hour are easy ways to spend time by yourself, like taking a bath or a longer-than-usual shower, going to get yourself a coffee instead of making one at home, going for a walk, or making time to journal. If you are feeling more adventurous you could take yourself on a date. Pick a place you like and set a time to meet yourself there. I used to love sitting alone in a restaurant watching people and getting lost in my thoughts. I learned so much about how I see the world and where I think my place in it is, and there's something so refreshing about not having to keep a conversation going or worrying that you've stayed there too long. That's not to say that it won't be uncomfortable at first, challenging even, but spending time alone is a great way to build this new relationship with yourself.

Anyone who knows me knows how much I value journaling. It has to be the single best thing we can do to get to know ourselves. But I also know that it can be hard to start. We can struggle with what we will say, if we will spell it all correctly, and if any of it will make sense, but none of that matters. When we journal we can see it as a way of dumping out all of the thoughts we are having onto paper. They most likely won't flow into a cohesive story, and we will probably be surprised where it takes us, but it's helpful for us to tap into the conversation that has been happening within us our whole lives.

A great place to start is to set a timer for five minutes and just write everything that comes to your mind. Even if you can't think of anything, actually write down, "I can't think of anything. What do I have to say?" The practice of noting this is that we're staying present with our thoughts so we can learn to start seeing who we truly are.

Another important piece on our journey to self-discovery is to try new things. As we get older we can, without realizing it, get stuck in our ways. Without giving it much thought we can say that we don't like that type of food, film, or activity. For the time being, let's pretend that we haven't tried anything. That we are being asked to go swimming for the very first time or to try a type of food we have never had before. To strip away all of the false beliefs we have created or ones that we have picked up from someone else, we have to be curious again. It is possible that we still don't like hiking, but let's give it a try and see what we find out. When we don't believe that we can take up space in our own life it's common for us to start living someone else's. We can do this through friendships, romantic relationships, and even work. Which is why we are going to need to double-check some of our assumptions.

When I was about ten years old my brother joined a ski club. He loved being on the mountain and would return from their trips already looking forward to the next one. I was almost four years younger and wanted to do everything my brother did, so as soon as I could, I learned how to ski. As I entered high school, snowboarding became more and more popular, and my friends kept trying to get me to switch over, to join their snowboarding groups, but I refused.

One thing you need to know about winter sports is that skiers and snowboarders haven't always gotten along. For many years, certain mountains only allowed skiers, and there was a belief that snowboarders ruined the snow, ran into people, and were just bad for mountain culture. Because snowboarding was relatively new at the time, their assumptions about it seemed true. Snowboarders did cut me off, plow the fresh powder, and were more dangerous on the mountain, but that was in part because they were all learning how to snowboard.

Flash forward about ten years and I meet my husband, Sean, who snowboards. He swears that I will love it and offers to teach me. I really liked Sean and wanted him to like me too, so I offered to learn. Other than the normal bumps and bruises that come along with learning a new skill, I did love it. The smoothness of riding down a mountain sideways, using your hips and body to carve your lines, felt easier somehow, more enjoyable. I haven't put on my skis in over fifteen years, and plan to buy a new snowboard again this winter. If I hadn't been open to trying something new, challenging this old belief I had about it, I would never have known just how much I could love snowboarding.

While this example might seem trivial, it's all part of how I continue to get to know myself. If I am not open to trying new things or questioning a belief that I have, I can start to lose sight of who I am. I also know that learning how to do new things and getting good at them helps build our self-esteem. It's that feeling I get when I can teach one of my friends how to snowboard, and they get the hang of it too. I am proud not only of my ability but also of my capacity to teach it to someone else. If I am going to try and speak up, assert myself, and take up space, I am going to have to feel more confident. Building this confidence has been hard for me, but learning to do new things has been a helpful shortcut.

I wish doing this work was a one-time thing. That we could learn why we are shrinking ourselves, address it once, and be done. But the reality is, it's an ongoing process. We have to continuously challenge old beliefs, try new things, and remind ourselves that we deserve to take up space. Each step forward, no matter how small, is a victory in reclaiming our right to exist fully and authentically. This journey of self-discovery and confidence-building is ongoing, but it's worth every effort because it leads to a more fulfilled and empowered life. It also allows us to more deeply connect with those around us in an authentic way, knowing who we are and using that knowledge to find others in our life to connect with and hold space for us to show up as we are.

"WHY DO I KEEP DOING THIS?" EXERCISE— *QUESTIONS TO IDENTIFY AND CHANGE THE URGE TO SHRINK YOURSELF*

1. What do you usually feel when you share what you are struggling with? When you are talking with others, how often do you feel like you might be talking too much?
2. When you find yourself sharing an emotion, especially ones like anger or sadness, what internal dialogue are you telling yourself about the experience?
3. What do you find most difficult about making decisions in your life? Do you struggle to decide or turn to others when making decisions?
4. Would you be able to do something on your own easily? Why or why not?
5. What are your feelings around the need to be productive? What happens when you don't have anything to do?
6. If you were writing a story and you were the main character, how would you describe yourself?

CONTROL CHALLENGE

Name the Part That Shrinks You

- Ask yourself: "What part of me holds back? What is it afraid of?"
- Write a few sentences from this part's perspective.

Choose One Expansion Challenge

Unapologetic share: Speak up in a conversation without minimizing or rushing yourself.

Bold decision: Make a decision without seeking reassurance.

Presence exercise: Stand or sit with an open, confident posture for two minutes.

Stillness challenge: Spend five minutes doing nothing and notice what comes up.

Reflect Briefly

- What felt uncomfortable?
- What surprised you?
- What did your shrinking part say?

Chapter 5

EMPATHY AND BEING OVERLY SENSITIVE

When Feeling for Others Leaves No Room for Ourselves

IMAGINE YOU'RE IN A CROWDED ROOM CHATTING WITH SOME friends, and the buzz of conversation envelops you. You look across the room and see your closest friend with her shoulders hunched forward and her eyes focused on the floor. Instinctively, you know something isn't right, so you excuse yourself and rush over to her. As you get closer she looks up and a tear slides down her cheek. You understand that she is upset and needs comforting, and you hug her. Without exchanging a single word, you recognize her pain. This is empathy—a profound connection that transcends language and touches the very core of our humanity.

Empathy is not just an abstract concept; it is the heartbeat of our interactions, the invisible thread that weaves us together in times of joy and sorrow. It is the silent acknowledgment that we are not alone in our struggles, that someone else feels our pain and shares our triumphs.

For years I have touted that I am an empathic badass, and that's because I do have a knack for reading people and situations, and knowing how to offer much-needed support. Empathy often feels like my superpower, allowing me to discern the next best move and swiftly navigate beyond surface-level conversations. It's why many of my friends turn to me in times of need, knowing that I will truly understand and provide genuine support. I can sit in the discomfort with them and do my best to understand their pain.

It has also been an invaluable tool in my career as a therapist, helping me to navigate and gently dismantle my patients' automatic defenses. I can often sense when something is off, whether they are lying or hiding a bigger issue. While I don't confront these observations directly, I tailor my questions to gently steer the conversation toward what I believe to be the real problem. This empathetic approach not only builds trust but also allows my patients to open up at their own pace, leading to deeper, more meaningful breakthroughs in their therapy.

TYPES OF EMPATHY

When discussing empathy, it's important to know that there are three distinct types: cognitive, emotional, and compassionate. Each type plays a crucial role in our relationships and interactions.

Cognitive empathy, also known as "perspective-taking," involves understanding another person's thoughts and emotions. It's about stepping into their shoes and seeing the world through their eyes. This type of empathy is essential in communication, as it allows us to comprehend why someone feels the way they do, even if we don't share their feelings. For example, cognitive empathy enables us to appreciate a friend's viewpoint during a disagreement. By understanding their perspective, we can find common ground and work toward a resolution that respects both of our viewpoints. Cognitive empathy helps us navigate complex social dynamics, fostering cooperation and mutual respect.

Emotional empathy, or "affective empathy," is the ability to physically feel what another person is experiencing. When we witness someone in distress, emotional empathy triggers an instinctive response within us, mirroring their emotions. This type of empathy is deeply rooted in our biology, and even fMRI (functional magnetic resonance imaging) shows that those of us with empathy "exhibit unconscious mimicry of the postures, mannerisms, and facial expressions of others to a greater degree than individuals who are unempathic." This means that if we watch someone fall down and skin their knee, the same motor and sensory areas affected by that fall are activated in our own brain. Emotional empathy is vital in personal relationships. When a friend is grieving, our ability to feel their sorrow allows us to provide genuine comfort and support. It creates a bond of shared experience, reinforcing the connection and trust between us.

Compassionate empathy, or "empathic concern," goes beyond understanding and sharing emotions. It involves taking action to help others in need. This type of empathy combines cognitive and emotional empathy with a proactive approach to alleviate another's suffering. In therapeutic settings, compassionate empathy is crucial. As a therapist, understanding a patient's struggles (cognitive empathy) and feeling their pain (emotional empathy) lays the groundwork for compassionate actions, such as providing tailored interventions and support. Compassionate empathy drives us to make a difference, whether by offering a listening ear, lending a helping hand, or giving professional guidance.

WITHOUT EMPATHY

Empathy is what makes us human. It's something we all need and allows us to form deep connections. However, not everyone experiences it. One of the key traits of narcissistic personality disorder (NPD) is "lack of empathy: [being] unwilling to recognize or identify with the feelings and needs of others." We also see this type of behavior in those with antisocial personality disorder (ASPD), but it's broader than just not experiencing empathy. Such people have "a pervasive pattern of disregard for and violation of the rights of others." For those of us who are empathic badasses, this can be confusing and tough to understand. Imagining a life where we don't consider others and aren't able to put ourselves in someone else's shoes just seems impossible.

It can be hard to wrap our heads around the fact that some people don't see others as humans with feelings. Instead, they see them as pieces in the chess game of life—something to manipulate, not connect with. It even feels wrong to write that, but for them, control is the goal, not emotional connection.

Those with NPD and ASPD often view others as tools to meet their own needs, which is why many people leave relationships with them feeling used and uncared for. They may have been involved with someone who is incapable of true empathy. Unfortunately, those of us who are highly empathetic—sometimes referred to as empaths—are particularly susceptible to these dynamics. Our deep care, kindness, and willingness to give are wonderful traits in a healthy relationship, but in the wrong hands they become an entry point for control.

For example, someone with ASPD will have an easier time persuading an empath to go along with their plans or believe their lies because they know we prioritize others' feelings. When we instinctively put others first, we can find ourselves agreeing to things just to keep the peace or make someone else happy—often without realizing we are being controlled. In the end, our empathy isn't the problem, it's how easily it can be used as a tool for manipulation.

Although we often think of narcissists as conceited people who can only think of themselves, they are also very scared, sad, and fragile. They need attention and validation from others to help regulate themselves, and in the psychology space we call that "supply." They need other people to supply them with enough love and admiration to make up for the fact that deep down they are fragile and unsure of who they are. Therefore, when a narcissist goes out looking for friends or romantic partners, they are going to try to find someone who can easily give them all of the validation and assurance they need. In short, empaths make the most desirable partners for a narcissist. This is why it's important to understand the dynamics and why we can feel drawn to those with NPD and ASPD. If it feels like they only take and take from us, it might be better to walk away.

TOXIC EMPATHY

While empathy is valuable for close relationships, it can sometimes become overactive and toxic. We might struggle to turn it off, pouring all our energy into others and ending up burnt out. Remember in the last chapter I mentioned that empathy has a role in feeling like too much. This is where this comes into play. The key issue with toxic empathy is our ability to set and maintain healthy boundaries. Boundaries allow us to care for others and ourselves; without them, we can lose sight of where we end and others begin.

If we don't have any boundaries in our relationships, we can find ourselves putting their needs first and controlling ours, always making sure they are healthy and happy, even if that means that we aren't. Over time our empathy can turn toxic, convincing us that our wants and needs don't matter as much because *someone else always has it worse*. In response, control steps in—not in the form of controlling others, but in controlling ourselves. We push our feelings aside, dismiss our own needs, and shrink ourselves to maintain harmony, mistaking self-denial for care. I hear this all the time from my community, just like this comment from Lydia:

> *I don't know what's wrong with me. I mean, nothing bad happened to me. I don't have trauma, my parents were okay, but I struggle every day to get up and get to work. I am constantly on edge, feel overwhelmed, and lately have started to wonder why I am even still here. I feel lost, but I don't want to reach out for help because there are so many people out there who have it worse. They deserve to get care way more than I do.*

When we deeply empathize with others, it can become difficult to leave space for our own pain and suffering. It's as if we believe that emotional support is like a cake with only so many slices to go around—by taking a slice for ourselves, we fear we're depriving someone else. But the truth is, there's an abundance of emotional "cake" to go around. Our pain is just as valid as anyone else's and acknowledging it doesn't diminish our ability to care for others. In fact, allowing ourselves to feel and process our own emotions can actually make us more compassionate and resilient, enabling us to offer more genuine support. Ignoring our own struggles doesn't make them disappear; it only adds to our emotional burden, leaving us depleted and less able to be present for those we care about.

Another unfortunate side effect of toxic empathy is when we catch other people's feelings like a virus. In a way, we are wired to do this, which is why it's so common. When we watch someone else in pain our brain and body can react as if it's happening to us. However, just feeling for others isn't what makes this piece toxic. It's when we are unable to distinguish between our own experience and that of those around us. It's almost like how we think and feel is hijacked by someone else's emotional response.

Just a few weeks ago I woke up in a good mood. It was nice; I was excited about the day and looking forward to the dinner plans my husband, Sean, and I had. Unfortunately, Sean woke up to some bad news. Our contractor wasn't getting things completed on time and had left yet another message with an excuse. I felt Sean's bad mood immediately and asked him what was wrong. He grumbled about the call and how upset it made him, and I felt myself get pulled into it too. My giddy demeanor drained from my body as I felt myself tense up and get angry. At that moment, I allowed Sean's bad mood to rub off onto me and accepted it as my own. I let my empathy for him and the situation become my experience, even though it wasn't.

While we all do that from time to time, it's important to recognize just how powerless it leaves us. It means that we are no longer in the driver's seat of our emotional experience, we are simply a passenger along for the ride.

Being unable to regulate our empathy can lead to emotional overload and complete burnout. It's something they try to beat into our brains as therapists. We have to leave work at work and not let a patient's struggle affect the rest of our day. Doing this is difficult but vital to our ability to continue doing our job without harming ourselves. We aren't made to hold everyone's pain, feel everything others feel, and still be able to live our lives. Doing so would be overwhelming. Even if we aren't working in a caretaker role, we have to protect ourselves from feeling things that aren't our own.

THE HIGHLY SENSITIVE PERSON

In 1997, Elaine N. Aron coined the term the "highly sensitive person," or HSP, to describe those of us who often feel overwhelmed by the world.[1] When defining an HSP, Aron shares that they are people who easily find themselves physically and emotionally overstimulated, often needing time to recharge in a dark and quiet space. HSPs are more sensitive to light, noise, and even pain than non-HSPs. They can find themselves deeply affected by other people's moods. Essentially, HSPs tend to experience life more intensely, processing the things around them with more depth, which can make everyday interactions feel overwhelming.

Because HSP was a new term, and many mental health professionals didn't know how to properly assess it, Aron created a helpful acronym and tool: DOES. The D stands for "depth of processing," because they find that HSPs tend to process things happening in their lives much more deeply than those who are not HSPs. This can mean that coming to a decision or moving past an upset can take us much longer. We can spend a lot of time thinking through every detail and emotion and relating it to earlier experiences. It's also common for us to hear that we are taking too long, overthinking things, and making it harder than it needs to be.

The thing to remember here is that when we are highly sensitive, it is part of our nature to process things more deeply. It's not necessarily a negative trait, but rather a different way of experiencing and interacting with the world. It can even be a gift, especially if our job requires us to pay attention to detail or create a specific feeling in a space. Being an HSP means that we get to use our depth of processing to our advantage and curate some amazing things.

However, if we are taking in all the minute details and considering not only ourselves but also everyone around us, we can easily become overstimulated. Which is why the O in DOES stands for "overstimulation." Processing every aspect of our surroundings means that we notice everything, and because our world is loud, busy, and nonstop, we can find ourselves shutting down. We often need to recharge before we can reengage with people, or we prefer certain spaces and ways of interacting. For example, one of my best friends is highly sensitive and hates overhead lighting. When she comes into my house she will instinctively turn off the ceiling lights and turn on a lamp. She says that having to focus in a room with bright overhead lights is like trying to sing your favorite song while another one is playing; it takes an increased effort and still doesn't come out right.

It's not just what we see and hear that can overwhelm us, we could find ourselves like Vanessa, a member of my community, who shares:

> *I honestly think I feel everything. Vibes, people's emotional responses, you name it. But the most distressing feeling for me is actually in the clothes that I wear. I can only wear clothing that is loose and made out of specific fabrics. I always check the seams of new clothes, making sure they are smooth and comfortable, and whenever I buy something new I immediately rip the tags out. I have this vivid memory as a child going to church for Easter Sunday in this taffeta dress that was so rough and itchy. I kept pulling at it, wanting to take it off, but my mom insisted I wear it and sit quietly. By the time church was over I was in a full meltdown. I ripped that dress off and sat in the car in my underwear. I was in so much trouble when I got home, but at least I wasn't stuck in that dress anymore.*

So much in our environment can overstimulate us when we are highly sensitive, because we can't help but absorb everything around us. Vanessa's heightened responses are a prime example of what the E in DOES stands for: "emotional reactivity." This means that HSPs like Vanessa experience emotions more intensely and react more strongly to stimuli, whether it's a loud noise, a strong smell, or even the emotions of those around them. Our heightened sensitivity makes us deeply empathetic and aware, but it also means we can easily become overwhelmed by our surroundings.

A sensitivity to subtleties—the S in the DOES acronym—is a core aspect of being an HSP. We are naturally attuned to the nuances in our environment, whether it's picking up on the slightest shift in someone's emotional state or noticing subtle sensory details that others might overlook. This heightened awareness is both a gift and a challenge. On one hand, it allows us to appreciate the richness and depth of our experiences, from the beauty in a simple moment to the complex emotions of those around us. We can be deeply empathetic, insightful, and creative because of this sensitivity.

However, this same sensitivity also means we are more easily overwhelmed by our surroundings. We might find crowded places, loud noises, or intense emotions particularly draining. The constant influx of stimuli can leave us feeling overstimulated or exhausted if we're not careful. Therefore, it's crucial for HSPs to be mindful of their limits and actively take steps to protect their well-being. This might involve setting boundaries, creating quiet spaces to recharge, or being selective about the environments and people we engage with.

Like most personality traits, empathy has its pluses and minuses. It can be wonderful to put ourselves in someone else's shoes, but if we do that with everyone, those experiences can quickly become too much. This is why many HSPs feel the need to take breaks from people and stimulating environments. It gives us a chance to recharge and relax before diving back in. I know I experience this when I'm in extreme social situations like conferences or conventions. After spending hours in such settings, I often need some quiet time alone to recover and regain my energy.

An important distinction to make when talking about being an HSP is that it's not the same as shyness. HSPs do enjoy the company of others, and like to socialize, we just have to do it carefully so that we don't get overstimulated. We also may need to spread out our social events so that we can recharge in between. It's all about modulating our lifestyle to fit our abilities.

Being able to tap into the potentiality of being highly sensitive is where our power lies. Sure, we can get bogged down by the ways it slows us down or causes us to feel dysregulated, but it also helps us navigate tricky situations with ease, utilizing our heightened awareness and empathy. This ability to perceive subtle changes in our environment and understand the emotions of others can be a tremendous asset. By embracing and managing our sensitivities, we can turn what might seem like a vulnerability into a unique strength, allowing us to connect deeply with others and make informed, thoughtful decisions.

IS IT INTUITION?

Have you ever walked into a room and immediately known something was off? A few years ago, I was heading to a girls' weekend, and because I had to work all day on Friday, I was going to be the last to arrive. When I got to our Airbnb, I immediately knew something was off. Everyone was quieter than usual, many had paired off, and each group was just doing their own thing. This wasn't what our group chat had discussed the day before. We were supposed to be playing a new card game tonight, making pizza, and enjoying the hot tub. Something had happened before I got there; I knew it in my bones.

I pulled aside my closest friend and asked her what was up. She quickly told me that it was too much to talk about right now, but that two of the other girls had gotten into a fight earlier in the day and neither had apologized. She said it was so awkward and uncomfortable that they all scattered and did their own thing, hoping this would give them time to cool down and move past it.

I hadn't been there when the fight took place, but when I walked into that house, I instinctively knew that something was wrong. My intuition told me that something was amiss, and without having any knowledge of what that was, I was able to tread lightly until I figured out the cause.

Our intuition is a powerful thing, and it doesn't only operate when things are going wrong; it can also tell us when something is meant for us and help us take that leap. It can be the push we need to take that new job or reach out and ask for what we want. It can also allow us to avoid situations that could do more harm than good. In many ways our intuition connects seamlessly with our empathy. Both work off of the unspoken, picking up on small movements, and even feeling the energy in a room. Together they can guide our lives, help us navigate difficult situations, and let us feel secure in the choices we make.

However, empathy and intuition are not always correct. They are often based on our own past experiences, and if we haven't had the easiest life, we might find ourselves making choices today influenced by those experiences. This means that our intuitive feelings and empathetic responses can sometimes be shaped by past traumas or biases, leading us to misinterpret current situations. Just like our empathy can turn toxic, so can our intuition. We have to be careful of reacting to it and making impactful decisions based on it. Instead, we should attune ourselves to its message and then check to see if it is rooted in fact or only in past experiences.

This isn't to say that our intuition is always wrong, either. There have been many instances where I knew in my gut that someone wasn't honest or a good person. I didn't have any facts to support this; it was just a feeling. So I kept my distance and trusted my intuition. Months later I found out that they had lied to some of my friends, had made false promises, and in some instances had even swindled them out of money. If I had ignored my intuition I could have fallen victim too.

Our intuition and empathy are powerful tools, guiding us through life by helping us make decisions, connect with others, and protect ourselves from harm. When these forces work together, they can create a strong internal compass that steers us toward what feels right and away from what might be damaging. However, it's important to remember that these instincts, while valuable, are not infallible. They are influenced by our past experiences, including any trauma or bias we've accumulated over time. This can sometimes lead us to misinterpret situations or react in ways that aren't entirely aligned with the present reality.

The challenge, then, is to learn how to discern when our intuition and empathy are guiding us correctly and when they might be clouded by our past. This requires a balance between trusting our gut and taking a step back to evaluate whether our instincts are rooted in current facts or old wounds.

WHO DO I LISTEN TO?

It's not uncommon for me to find myself stuck and unable to make a decision because I worry how it will make someone else feel. My empathy hijacks my brain, and it won't allow me to move forward for fear that it will put someone else in a precarious situation. It's those times that my intuition seems to be on vacation, not giving me a direct feeling or guiding light. I can feel lost, afraid, and unsure of what to do next.

This can last for days, even weeks sometimes, when I don't know what to do. It's a hopeless place to be when you know you need to do something, but you just aren't sure what it is. And I am just going to say it, the pros and cons lists don't do shit in situations like this. I know therapists can push us to create such lists, thinking that it will somehow help with tough decisions, but when we are caught in this Bermuda Triangle of assessment, it only muddies the water.

What I have learned through years of therapy and journaling is that it's not the decision itself that is complicated. It's that what I know I need to do will require more courage than I have at the moment. It stresses me out, and because I don't feel able to take the action needed, I freeze. This realization, while it can seem so obvious, was a game changer for me. Instead of focusing on the issue of what to do, I could focus on what I needed at the moment to feel more courageous and ready to take the action that was best for me. That small shift, time and time again, seems to thaw me out, and I can step into the next phase without having a complete meltdown.

Reframing is one of the magic tools used in therapy. It's a way to change our focus, from something that is keeping us stuck to something else that can help us move forward. Sometimes when we are stuck or struggling with something, we look for the solution or the way to "fix" it, oftentimes leading to controlling behavior. Instead, we should be looking at what's causing us to feel stuck in the first place. Shifting our focus can open up a new lane, one full of possibilities, that's not fraught with fear and misplaced empathy. It can also take the pressure off the decision itself and our urge to control every part of it.

This shift in focus can help us put some distance between ourselves and the action we need to take, and that's often all we need to see things clearly. Which is why it's important to have space between ourselves and others. Not a ton of space, but enough that we don't get so clouded by their emotions that we can't tell what's ours.

STOP BEING A SPONGE

Boundaries are always going to be an empath's best friend. When we find ourselves controlled by other people's reactions to life, we are going to have to find ways to see ourselves without the influence of others. That can be difficult. Like I mentioned in chapter 3, enmeshment and codependency are incredibly common and can make it feel wrong to create space between us and those we love.

If you find yourself thinking and feeling that way, like I did, one tool that has helped me keep other people's emotions out of my head is to consider the origin.

When I start feeling different—let's say I was feeling hopeful or happy and suddenly I feel disappointed—I need to see if I can figure out where that emotion came from. Did someone around me express this to me? Did I read something upsetting? Did I see something online that didn't align with my thoughts or values? We have to take a minute to consider the source. Too often I find it came from something so trivial that it's embarrassing.

Last week I woke up feeling fine, tired but good. I brushed my teeth, washed my face, made breakfast, and took the dog for a walk. When I got back, I felt a sense of not being good enough. It was like a wave; it just came over me and stole my motivation for work. I paused and considered: Where did this feeling come from? I hadn't done anything yet, so how could something have influenced me already? As I thought through my morning, I realized that it was because while I was eating breakfast, I looked through social media and saw a woman sharing how she had found her husband cheating on her. It was devastating but had nothing to do with me. I don't know this person, wasn't involved in this story in any way, yet I was allowing her emotional reaction to impact my day.

It's important to realize that these emotions can affect us from a distance, and it can help to consider where they came from. Once I realized that it wasn't my own emotion, I had to mentally detangle myself from it. I do this by checking my facts.

This is a great cognitive behavioral therapy (CBT) tool—going through only the facts about a situation, not our thoughts or feelings about it. And just in case you were wondering, having a thought multiple times doesn't make it a fact, either. In this case, it looked like me asking what happened, whether or not I had any control over her situation, and if I needed to be involved. The answer is that I had no control, it was not my problem to solve, and if I tried to butt in, it would be odd and unhealthy.

The reason I love this CBT tool so much is because it cuts through all of the intense emotions we can feel when we are empathic and allows us to see what took place, nothing more. It forces me to recognize the truth, not just what I have told myself or built up in my mind. That's the trap with empathy; it starts out good and caring, but we can give ourselves more responsibility and power than is accurate. I can't help everyone, I shouldn't butt into other people's issues, and I am not responsible for anyone's happiness other than my own.

WHERE DO I NEED BOUNDARIES?

Creating enough space to check our facts can be tricky. Being able to set boundaries between our feelings and those of the people around us is key to creating that space. The good news is that we don't have to create this space everywhere and with everyone. It's only in situations where we can't tell what emotional experience is ours versus someone else's. Another telltale sign of a need to create boundaries is if we feel drained after spending time with someone or find ourselves trying to avoid them altogether. The urge to steer clear of someone usually comes from a need to create space between ourselves and others. This could look like letting someone know that we need to have time to share our upsets instead of only listening to theirs. Or it could mean that we can't be available all the time.

Some of these boundaries will need to be communicated directly, while others can be enforced through actions. For example, if our problem is that we allow one of our friends to call us anytime, and they consistently wake us up in the middle of the night, then the boundary would be to put our phone on silent and go to sleep. Not picking up after we have gone to bed is the boundary, and by acting in that way, we are enforcing it. As a reminder, boundaries are not requests that we place with other people, they are things that we do to keep that healthy space. We don't have control over anyone else, so we have to keep our focus on ourselves and what we can do.

If you're anything like me, you struggle to tell what emotions are yours in most of your relationships. While that can sound like it makes our issue way worse, it really doesn't. What I learned is that when this is happening with everyone, it doesn't have anything to do with the relationships; it has to do with me. The way I was interacting with my friends and family was creating an unhealthy dynamic. I would never share how I was feeling, always turning the conversation back to them, doing what I could to cater to their needs even when they didn't expressly ask for it. Because I was so focused on everyone else's emotions, I never checked in on my own, and often took on the emotions of those around me as a priority, making sure I was showing up for them first.

Doing this repeatedly for years meant that most of my relationships were based on this type of behavior. My outward focus on everyone else made it easy to blur the lines between my own emotions and theirs, making it hard to tell the difference. No one asked me how I was doing because I never shared. Since I would always go out of my way to accommodate them, they never had the chance to do that for me. Again, it's like I tied myself up and then complained about the constraints. I had to change the way that I allowed people to be in my life. I had to allow others to show up for me, and then sit with the discomfort of being cared for.

ALLOWING FOR CARE

Being cared for sounds nice and easy, but if you've spent most of your life prioritizing the feelings and needs of others while neglecting your own, it can feel incredibly uncomfortable. The idea of someone else taking care of you can stir up feelings of guilt, vulnerability, or even inadequacy, as if accepting help makes you less capable or strong. However, learning to let others show up for you is a crucial part of building healthy, reciprocal relationships.

The first step is recognizing that it's okay to receive care without immediately giving something in return. Start small by accepting compliments, gestures of kindness, or offers of help without feeling the urge to deflect or reciprocate right away. If someone tells you they like your outfit, simply say thank you. Resist saying something to brush off the compliment. Practice sitting with the discomfort that might arise, reminding yourself that allowing others to care for you doesn't diminish your worth—it honors your humanity.

Over time, we can disconnect ourselves from the belief that our value is tied solely to what we can offer others. Instead, we can focus on building trust in our relationships, where care and support flow both ways. This process involves being honest about our needs and vulnerabilities and allowing others to meet us where we are.

I have been working on this for years, and trust me when I tell you that you will gradually become more comfortable with receiving and will likely find that your relationships deepen and become more balanced. You'll no longer feel the pressure to overcompensate or to constantly be the giver. Instead, you can enjoy the mutual exchange of care and connection, which strengthens bonds and allows for more authentic, supportive interactions.

Ultimately, allowing ourselves to be cared for is an act of self-compassion. It's acknowledging that we deserve the same kindness and attention we so readily offer to others. By embracing this, we create space for more meaningful and fulfilling relationships where everyone involved can thrive.

DEALING WITH THE GUILT

When we first start allowing others to show up for us, it can come along with some feelings of guilt. We can think that by sharing how rough of a week we had we are overburdening someone we love. But I encourage you to stick with it. Check your facts and see if they said it was too much or asked you to stop sharing such intense information. We need to trust those we love enough to know that they will speak up for themselves, tell us when we have overstepped, and allow us to correct our actions. Reading minds isn't something we are capable of, and we have to stop pretending that we can.

Guilt kept me stuck in these patterns far longer than I care to admit, perpetuating how I was controlling my own feelings, but through trial and error, I found a technique that actually works. Instead of allowing our deep empathy to intensify the guilt, we can use it to gain a clearer perspective.

Think about how you'd respond if a friend needed to take a break or ask for help, even if you were busy. You likely wouldn't judge or think less of them. In fact, you'd probably be understanding and willing to support them. By imagining ourselves in their shoes, we see how misplaced our guilt is. If the situation were reversed, we'd offer compassion rather than frustration, revealing that our guilt is often unnecessary.

Letting go of the inappropriate guilt takes time and practice, but I have found it to be the best way to free myself from the trap I unknowingly set. It's a process of gradually rewiring my thoughts, permitting myself to prioritize my own needs, and recognizing that I'm worthy of the same compassion I extend to others. Over time, this shift has allowed me to find more enjoyment in my relationships and see my empathy as a useful tool instead of my entire personality.

FINDING BALANCE

Empathy is a powerful force that connects us deeply with others, allowing us to share in their joys and sorrows. Yet, like any strength, it requires balance. When we allow empathy to overextend or when we feel too deeply for others, we risk losing ourselves in the process. It's in these moments that healthy boundaries become essential—not as barriers to connection, but as safeguards for our emotional health.

Remember that setting boundaries isn't about withholding care; it's about ensuring that we have the space to care for ourselves as well. Intuition can guide us, but without boundaries, it can lead us into emotional exhaustion. It's okay to step back, to receive care without guilt, and to recognize that our needs are just as valid as those of the people we love.

"WHY DO I KEEP DOING THIS?" EXERCISE— *QUESTIONS TO IDENTIFY AND MANAGE THE URGE TO BE OVERLY EMPATHIC*

1. How often do you find yourself "catching" someone else's emotional experience or feeling something and not knowing where it came from?
2. How confident are you with your empathy and intuition? Are there areas where you feel these might be influenced by your past experiences?
3. In what situations do you find yourself needing time to recharge after spending time around other people?
4. Describe your experience with sharing your struggles with others. How often do you feel guilty or feel like you owe them?

5. What types of boundaries do you find to be the most difficult to identify and set? Why?
6. Are there ways you could try and put yourself first? What would that look like?

CONTROL CHALLENGE

Identify an emotion: Think of a recent situation where you felt strongly for someone else (anger, sadness, guilt, etc.).

Check the facts—ask yourself:

- "What actually happened in this situation?" (Not what you felt or thought about it.)
- "Do I have any control over this person's situation?"
- "Is this my problem to solve?"
- "Is this emotion mine, or did I absorb it from someone else?"

Refocus: After answering these questions, separate your emotions from theirs. Remind yourself: "I am not responsible for anyone's happiness other than my own."

Chapter 6

NUMBING OUT AND DISCONNECTING

The Endless Things We Do to Not Feel Uncomfortable

We all have moments when the weight of discomfort feels like too much to bear. Whether it's the sting of stress, the ache of loneliness, or the nagging hum of anxiety, we instinctively reach for something—anything—to dull the pain, to control how much we're feeling. These escapes come in many forms, each offering its own kind of relief or reprieve from what we would rather not feel. For some, it's pouring a drink and letting the alcohol blur the edges of a difficult day. For others, it's the rush of buying something new, a fleeting thrill that momentarily fills the emptiness. Some of us dive into the digital world, scrolling endlessly through social media or binge-watching TV shows to avoid facing what's going on inside.

These behaviors can feel like lifelines in moments of distress, but they often come at a cost. What starts as an innocent distraction can quickly turn into a habit, controlling how much we pull away from the very feelings we need to confront. Just like in this example from Amber:

> *I have been someone who has always felt every emotion very deeply, not only my own emotions but those of others as well. Feeling deeply is exhausting and sometimes my body is grasping at ways to get a break from working so hard for me. Unfortunately, these ways are not always good. Just like lots of others, I numb out by looking at my phone and feeling like I can't stop getting immersed in social media, online shopping, and videos. My mind also has reverted to self-harm and disordered eating behaviors. These "coping skills" unfortunately cause more problems. They may relieve me for a short time, but they also cause the continued cycle of depression and anxiety and oftentimes negatively affect those around me as well. Finding healthier ways to get relief I hope can one day break the painful cycle.*

What Amber describes is something we all experience. We each have our own ways of controlling difficult emotions and the challenges we face, and it's understandable. Feeling everything can be overwhelming, so we instinctively reach for the easiest distraction we can find. What we reach for can even change depending on the situation. When we feel excited we may want to overeat, when we are sad we may want to have another glass of wine, or when we're angry we may find ourselves mindlessly scrolling on social media. The possibilities are endless, all aimed at avoiding our true feelings when confronting them directly feels too difficult.

PICK YOUR POISON

While there are countless ways to numb and control our emotions, some methods are more common than others. The one I see the most is numbing out by watching television or scrolling through social media. Many of us even do these two things at the same time. We will have a show on in the background while we see what we missed on our favorite social media app. This is most common because it's so accessible and seems pretty benign.

While it doesn't directly cause another mental health issue, it doesn't allow us to feel anything, either. It pulls our focus away from ourselves and what we are going through and distracts us with someone else's life or story. Social media can also give us a place to vent our frustrations on others without directly taking responsibility for it. We can get online when we feel angry and lash out at strangers via the comments, taking out our frustrations on people we don't even know. We can jump into the comments to correct someone when we aren't feeling seen or heard in our own life, and for a brief second feel vindicated. We can use social media as a dumping ground for the emotions we should be communicating in real life.

Social media can be a great place to genuinely connect with others, but it's also important to recognize whether we're using it to build relationships or if we're simply using it to escape or distract ourselves. I use this to numb out quite often, but I didn't realize it until I had tried journaling daily and started to notice a pattern. Whenever I would sit down in the morning to journal, I would feel pulled to my phone. One minute I am trying to figure out why I have been feeling so alone lately, and the next I am laughing at a meme my friend sent me. It is a great escape, and I still struggle to pull myself away from it. It's so bad that I have to leave my phone in another room when I journal so that I don't distract myself from how I am feeling.

Another common way to numb ourselves is through overfunctioning. This can show up as immersing ourselves in work or other productive activities to avoid confronting our emotions. The challenge with this behavior is that our society often praises it, celebrating what is popularly known as "hustle culture." We get rewarded for controlling, thereby ignoring our emotions when we receive a promotion or are compensated for working harder, which reinforces that our focus on overachieving is "benefiting" us. But when these accolades come at the cost of our true feelings and needs, or are used to avoid experiencing our emotions, it's not healthy or worth it.

Overfunctioning often intertwines with other perfectionistic behaviors, like excessive exercise. I had an unhealthy relationship with exercise, but it wasn't until my dad passed away that I truly grasped how severe it was. Exercise is often praised, with regular exercisers viewed as being disciplined, healthy, and in control of their lives. In my case, I was running almost every day, constantly pushing myself to go farther. I wasn't in control as much as I was trying to control how I felt. As my dad's health declined, no amount of running felt like enough. I forced myself to run daily, even when I was exhausted or in pain. After he passed, I broke down during an evening run, overwhelmed with grief. Despite my being physically and emotionally drained, a voice inside insisted I keep going, convincing me there was no time to rest. I was chasing that runner's high, desperately trying to numb the pain I couldn't face.

Shopping can also be a way to disconnect. For those with impulse control issues, it can quickly spiral out of control. I had a former patient who struggled with this, sometimes spending thousands of dollars in a single weekend. The challenge with this coping mechanism is that it does make us feel better, especially when we're dealing with sadness. Shopping provides a boost in dopamine, the hormone responsible for pleasure, satisfaction, and motivation. It can also give us a sense of control over our environment. We get to choose and purchase what we want, momentarily regaining a sense of agency and control in our lives. However, this mood lift is often fleeting and may fade even before the purchased items arrive, leading us to repeat the cycle.

Getting caught in this pattern can be incredibly harmful. We might end up in debt, struggling to pay our bills, or even hiding our purchases from our partners to avoid conflict. Essentially, our attempt to ignore our emotions creates even more problems. That's why it's important to be mindful of our shopping habits—are we genuinely enjoying the rewards of our hard work, or are we using shopping to numb our feelings? I also find it helpful to delay a purchase for twenty-four hours to see if I still want it or if it was just an emotional impulse.

Another common way to disconnect is by using drugs and alcohol. Here's a story from a member of my community sharing his struggle with this:

> *For me, my drug use was mostly cocaine. After we lost our baby, my partner kind of turned on me. I think she blamed me somehow. Now I was really feeling alone. Almost like when I was a child losing my parents. The cocaine seemed to erase the alone feeling in several ways. One is the outright euphoric feeling from the drug itself. Numbs the pain and grief for me. But a side effect is it made me not be so quiet and withdrawn. As if it unlocked the real me and put the beat-up, weathered, and worn me in the closet. I would be the life of the party where normally I would not dare to say hello to most people I didn't know. Eventually, however, the honeymoon with cocaine ends. The negatives start outweighing the positives. And the coming down always brought me lower than when I started.*

Like other methods of distancing ourselves and controlling our true feelings, using substances like drugs and alcohol may offer temporary relief but ultimately leave us feeling worse. Over time, this behavior can lead to dependency, making it difficult to stop even when we no longer want to disconnect. The consequences can be far-reaching, affecting our physical and mental health, jeopardizing our ability to hold a job, and damaging our relationships. What starts as a way to cope can quickly turn into a cycle that disrupts every aspect of our lives.

Similarly, people often turn to food as a means of control, numbing out because it provides immediate comfort, whether through overeating or undereating. Overeating can create a temporary sense of fullness that distracts from emotional pain, while undereating might offer a false sense of control in an otherwise chaotic world. Both behaviors serve as coping mechanisms to avoid confronting difficult emotions. Eating is particularly soothing because the act of sucking and swallowing stimulates the vagus nerve, which plays a key role in calming our nervous system. This is why certain dishes are referred to as "comfort foods"—they're warm, rich, and calming. They genuinely provide comfort, often leading us to eat more than we're truly hungry for. This physical response can make eating feel like an effective way to self-soothe, even though it ultimately doesn't address the underlying emotional issues.

Another less-discussed way to disconnect is through self-injury. While many other coping mechanisms also harm our bodies, this is a more direct form of self-harm. People may scratch, cut, or burn themselves as a way to avoid emotional pain. It can also help shift the focus from emotional pain to physical pain, which for some may be easier to tolerate and manage. Over my years as a therapist, both in person and online, I've seen this behavior with increasing frequency. Though some may find it difficult to understand why someone would hurt themselves, it's similar to other coping strategies—it's a form of control and provides temporary relief from intense or uncomfortable emotions.

In my teenage years, I started "doodling" with a razor blade. But it stirred some attention from a mentor in my life. I had so much love and respect for her that seeing her so upset about the design on top of my hand was enough for me to not do that anymore... well, I convinced her of that anyhow. I moved to doing it at the

> *top of my legs where no one could see (way above my shorts line). I remember doing it so that I would feel the physical pain instead of the emotional pain. It got my brain to turn off in a sense.*

Like many of these behaviors, self-injury can feel good because it triggers the release of endorphins, hormones that help relieve pain, reduce stress, and elevate our mood. This physical response can make the act seem rewarding, even though it offers only short-term relief and can lead to long-term harm. In essence, it gives us a momentary sense of control and relief, but at a significant cost to our well-being.

The final numbing behavior I frequently encounter is daydreaming and dissociation. I group these because daydreaming can be seen as a milder form of dissociation, with both serving as ways to control our reality by taking a break from it. When we feel overwhelmed, we might find ourselves spacing out more often, fantasizing about a vacation or even an entirely different life. Daydreaming offers a safe escape from stress, providing a mental break. Dissociation, on the other hand, is more extreme, acting as a way to detach from our body or environment. I often describe dissociation as the brain's way of pulling the rip cord on reality, temporarily tugging us away so we don't have to be fully present during difficult times. However, both forms of disconnecting prevent us from fully experiencing our lives and emotions, keeping us from living in the moment.

BUT IT FEELS BETTER

Given that each of these common disconnection tactics carries its own harmful side effects, it might seem irrational that we continue to use them. However, it's important to remember that they provide a temporary break from our emotions, and some even improve our mood in the short term. That's why we keep turning to them whenever we feel uncomfortable with the way we feel.

In many ways, we can attribute this to our biology. Our brain and body are wired to keep us alive, no matter what. When something harmful happens, they release hormones to lessen the pain. When we try to regain control, our dopamine levels rise, making us feel better. And when all else fails, our brain can pull the rip cord on reality, offering a much-needed mental escape. These natural responses are designed to protect us and ensure our survival, but they can backfire when we rely on them to avoid feeling our emotions. Over time, this reliance can prevent us from fully processing our experiences and truly living our lives.

When we repeatedly turn to unhealthy coping mechanisms like self-injury, overexercising, or compulsive shopping to avoid discomfort, we're not solving the underlying issue. Instead, we're burying it, pushing our emotions deeper into our bodies where they remain unprocessed. These unresolved emotions don't just disappear—they linger, often manifesting as physical symptoms such as chronic pain, tension, or digestive issues. Our body holds on to the emotional weight we refuse to address, and over time, this can lead to more serious health problems.

While these tactics might offer short-term relief by numbing our emotions or giving us a temporary sense of control, the long-term consequences can be damaging. The unprocessed emotions don't go away; they simply get stored in our body, waiting to be released.

WHY WE DON'T WANT TO FEEL

Feeling our feelings sounds natural and is obviously something we should all be doing, but in practice it can be incredibly difficult. The reason it can be so grueling is that many of us were never taught how to manage all that we feel. We could have been told that our emotions were too much for other people to handle. Over time we can think that something is wrong with us, that our emotional experience is wrong, and we have to stuff it down, control, and forget about it entirely. Giving ourselves permission to experience all that comes up can feel like admitting that something is wrong with us, and that's often too much to bear.

This belief that something must be wrong with us for having varied emotional responses to life stems from our deep-rooted judgment of emotions as a whole. If I told you that I was feeling all sorts of good emotions, which ones come to mind? Now consider if I told you I was feeling bad, what feelings do you think of? Without giving it too much thought, the most common responses are that happy, excited, or joyful are good emotions to feel and we should all experience them more often. On the other hand, anger, sadness, or fear are often considered to be bad feelings that should be avoided. We internalize these judgments, believing that if we experience the "bad" emotions, something is inherently wrong with us. This can cause us to question our emotional experiences rather than accepting them as natural human responses to life's complexities.

As a result, we develop a tendency to suppress, deny, or hide emotions that don't fit the idealized mold of constant happiness or calm. When we experience grief, anger, or anxiety, we may feel like we're failing in some way, which only adds a layer of shame or guilt to what we're already feeling. The reality is that our emotions are varied and fluid for a reason—they reflect the full spectrum of human experience. Allowing ourselves to experience it all means we can't cherry-pick specific feelings to acknowledge and ignore the rest. We have to let the emotions take us where they need to go, and that can be terrifying.

Letting ourselves feel every emotion can bring up intense vulnerability. If we're caught feeling sad or lonely, we might worry that others could take advantage of us or think less of us as a result. We may even feel more susceptible to other people's responses, and to protect ourselves from that, we often prefer not to go through it at all. Instead, we put up a tough exterior, pretend everything is okay, and press on. This has been my reason for stuffing things down—because I don't always know if I can handle the feedback I might receive in response to my emotions.

For example, I have recently shared more of myself and my process online. Not because I enjoy it, but because I think it's important for people to know that I am human too and we all go through rough patches in life. Essentially, I am hoping to showcase a more realistic life experience, rather than sugarcoating it or acting like I always have the answers. However, when I do this, I inevitably receive feedback I cannot take. People claim that I am making it up, shooting multiple takes so that I cry at the right part, and overall being a fraud. Even though I know everything I put out is authentic, that still hurts me deeply and has made sharing uncomfortable experiences and emotions much more difficult. I haven't done it since.

This is another reason why we can prefer to numb out. It can feel threatening to put it all out there. Our nervous system is wired to constantly evaluate our environment, searching for potential threats to our safety, whether physical or emotional. When it detects something it perceives as harmful, it triggers our stress response, preparing us to take action. This response is designed to protect us by getting us out of the threatening situation, which is why we often choose to avoid and control our emotions rather than confront them. We either run away from them or push them down, believing it's safer to keep everything hidden.

TAKING BACK THE RIGHT KIND OF CONTROL

Disconnecting can also feel like a way of taking back control rather than performing the controlling behavior, allowing us to choose when and how we deal with our emotions rather than letting them dominate our lives. We might even take pride in this ability, telling ourselves—and others—that instead of feeling sad, we went to the gym or threw ourselves into work. Society often praises this approach, equating it with strength and success. We may start to believe that pushing through and ignoring our feelings makes us stronger or more resilient. But of course, we'd be wrong.

I see and hear people talking about it like this all the time, with quotes being shared online like this one, from Paulo Coelho: "You have two choices: to control your mind or to let your mind control you."[1]

While I do agree that we shouldn't let our minds or emotions run the show, controlling them may be the wrong word to use here. As we've learned, we can't control our emotional responses to life; they happen with or without our consent and are a healthy part of our life experience. However, we can seek to understand them and then choose how to engage with them as they happen. One of my favorite quotes about feelings comes from Tim Robbins's character in the movie *Thanks for Sharing*: "Feelings are like children. You don't want them driving the car, but you shouldn't stuff them in the trunk either."

When we numb out, it's like shoving our emotions into the trunk—out of sight, out of mind. But what we need is to keep them in the backseat, where we can hear them and attend to them as needed. If we keep stuffing emotions away, eventually the trunk will overflow. When we try to add just one more, all those unresolved feelings will come spilling out, overwhelming us with emotions we've ignored for too long.

CRYING FOR NO REASON

When we habitually reach for distractions like the remote, a bottle of wine, or our phone instead of acknowledging our feelings, we risk becoming deeply disconnected from our own emotions. This pattern of numbing out can progressively distort our emotional awareness, making it challenging to pinpoint the origins of our feelings. Over time, this avoidance strategy creates a significant gap between our internal experiences and our external responses. This can then spill out into how we're showing up in our lives and in our relationships.

By continuously suppressing our emotions, we are essentially placing them in a pressure cooker, building up internal tension that has no outlet. Just like a pressure cooker that eventually needs to release steam, our emotions eventually demand to be expressed. However, because we've been avoiding them, we often lack the skills or awareness to manage them effectively when they do surface.

This buildup can lead to emotional outbursts or feelings of anxiety, sadness, or irritability appearing at inconvenient or inappropriate times. For instance, a minor disagreement with a friend can trigger an excessive emotional reaction because of the underlying unresolved feelings that have been simmering beneath the surface. Similarly, small stressors might provoke overwhelming anxiety or sadness because we've been ignoring the accumulation of these feelings for so long.

The problem with this emotional buildup is that it doesn't just vanish; it often erupts in ways that are disproportionate to the immediate trigger. When emotions are not processed or addressed as they arise, they accumulate and can lead to a dramatic overflow, impacting our behavior and interactions in ways we might later regret. This can result in strained relationships, damaged reputations, or unnecessary conflict, as the emotions we've been controlling and suppressing spill out unpredictably.

Moreover, this cycle of suppression and eruption reinforces the very controlling habits we are trying to avoid. Each time we try to control our emotions, we may inadvertently strengthen the pattern of avoidance, leading to even greater emotional disconnection and more frequent outbursts. In essence, our attempts to control and hide our emotions often backfire, making them more volatile and less manageable.

COMPLETE DISCONNECTION

While it can feel good not to endure specific emotions or experience something fully in the moment, over time this repression disconnects us from ourselves. If we don't know how something made us feel, it's going to be difficult to make decisions for ourselves because we don't have any history to base it on. If we spend our entire lives trying to minimize any negative emotions, we can lose touch with our authentic selves. We can feel like we don't know who we are, and maybe never have.

This disconnection can cause a range of other side effects. Without being in touch with our emotions, we miss out on opportunities for personal growth. Emotions often serve as important signals that highlight areas where we need to develop or change. By ignoring or suppressing them, we avoid confronting these challenges and, as a result, miss out on the chance to learn from our experiences. This lack of emotional engagement can stagnate our personal development and prevent us from reaching our full potential, ultimately impacting our ability to lead a fulfilling and self-aware life.

When we are disconnected from our emotions it can cause us to miss out on meaningful relationships or even engage with people who don't truly align with who we are, simply because we lack a strong foundation for choosing our connections. For example, when I returned to therapy after a long break, I discovered that I needed to reevaluate or even end certain relationships. As I started to reconnect with my true self, I realized that the people I spent time with while I was disconnected no longer felt like a good fit. This journey of getting back in touch with myself made it clear that there was a mismatch between who I really am and the relationships I maintained during those times of emotional detachment.

Without our emotions, we aren't able to fully experience life, know who we are, and grow into the best version of ourselves. This is why it's important to learn how to reconnect with our feelings, explore what they reveal about us, and use this understanding to guide our personal development.

TAPPING IN

I love this quote from Gabor Maté: "It's not about feeling better, it's about getting better at feeling."[2] Feeling our feelings sounds like it would be natural. We can think that if we want to engage with our emotional experience, we should be able to do so without much effort. Unfortunately, that's not the case. It is natural for our brain and body to feel our feelings easily, but we often don't know how to do it if we've been taught not to or have avoided them for most of our lives. I see posts online all the time from other mental health professionals about how important feeling your feelings is. The comments are always filled with people agreeing and then asking how they can make it happen. It took me quite a few years to figure this out, and I still find myself disconnecting from time to time. Know that with practice it is possible and it does get easier.

It's important to realize that emotions aren't about feeling, they are about doing. Our emotions motivate us to do something in the present. If we feel excited because our best friend is coming to visit, we are having that emotion because we are longing for that attachment. Our excitement gets us ready to connect and gain fulfillment from this important relationship. If we feel angry because someone took our idea at work and passed it off as their own, this emotion is protective. It tells us that we can't trust that person and encourages avoidance-type behavior. Whatever emotions we are experiencing, it's helpful to remember that they are there to initiate something.

As you recall, our nervous system is wired to look for any threat in our environment. The way it tells us about these potential threats is through our emotional responses. Emotions are our brain and body's messengers. They tell us when something is off or when we need more of something, and then they help guide us toward safely getting what we need.

Recognizing the role of emotions in my body was a game changer for me because I had spent years trying to figure out how to feel them, believing that was their only role. Thinking that I needed to set aside hours to let myself cry because I never did that or maybe I should go to one of those rage rooms where you get to break everything so that I could get my anger out. I believed that emotions needed to be released or expelled in some way. I pushed myself to find quick solutions, which didn't honor the reason the emotion existed at that moment. It's almost like my hurried efforts to move through them meant that I wasn't letting myself feel them at all.

As someone who tends to overfunction in life, I see this pattern everywhere. I constantly seek to understand a problem, figure out how to fix it, and then rush toward that goal. This pattern has me trying to think through my feelings instead of actually feeling them, also known as "intellectualizing." I believe that if I just do what I'm supposed to do to reach the goal, the discomfort will fade, and I can move on to the next thing. But this approach always leaves me frustrated, criticizing myself, and still feeling bad. When it comes to emotions, I can't control them or make them disappear by intellectualizing them. I need to recognize their presence, acknowledge the message they are sending, allow for them to be there without judging, and then learn from them. And I have to be honest—there's nothing more uncomfortable for me than doing that.

The next step in learning to feel our feelings is to get better at identifying them. I will never forget when one of my friends just got out of a therapy session. She met me for dinner and shared that her homework was to start identifying her emotions. She showed me the paper her therapist gave her, which was filled with emotion words, and lamented that it didn't have what she was feeling listed on it. I scanned the paper quickly and then asked her what emotion she was looking for. She thought for a second and said she wanted to be able to circle "numb" because that's how she truly felt. I had to stop myself from laughing because she was being sincere. I gently told her that numb wasn't a feeling, it was the absence of feelings. At first she was shocked, tried to argue that it was, and in the end realized she had a lot of work left to do.

When we've been ignoring our emotions for a long time, it can be challenging to identify what we're actually feeling. We might be unsure of our emotions, and even if someone tries to explain them, confusion can still linger. If any of that resonates, we can turn to reality television to help. I know that might come as a shock, but when we are trying to learn about emotions it can help to see them acted out. Reality television is one way to see these emotions in a more dramatic way, so the emotional responses are harder to miss. Watch for about ten minutes and then try to jot down some of the emotions you saw being demonstrated. This can help us better understand what each emotion looks like, how it can be expressed, and what can cause it.

Once you get the hang of noticing what emotions you see being communicated, ask yourself, how do you know it's that emotion? For example, if we see someone arguing with another person and we write down that we witnessed an expression of anger, how did we come to that conclusion? This can help us recognize how emotions are conveyed, whether it's through language, body movements, or even facial expressions. Knowing these things can help us begin to identify our own emotions when they come up.

LOOK FOR ANOTHER WAY IN

Says Quinn:

> *I don't even know where to start. I feel nothing, and my therapist keeps asking me to identify it or explain where I feel it in my body, and I just feel like an idiot. I have no answers for her so I sit there like a moron. Help!*

If you, like Quinn, still feel lost and have no idea how to identify emotions when they happen inside you, we can try another way in. As a therapist, I have always described that helping my patients can sometimes feel like trying to break into a house. While many people will just open the front door, let you in, and tell you what's going on with them, others are not that easy. Some people don't feel safe letting anyone in, and so we have to approach our entry from another angle. We may have to see if there's a back door or side window open and try going through there. That's what we are doing here—taking a different approach in the hope that this will get us inside our emotional experience.

First, see if you can identify your go-to behavior for disconnecting. The ones I mentioned earlier are by no means an exhaustive list and are just a starting point. What do you do when you feel discomfort? Start paying attention to your behaviors throughout the day and see if you can pinpoint one or more of these numb-outs. Knowing what we do to disconnect will inevitably tell us when we are feeling something. In essence, we are trying to break in through the back door.

Once we recognize a numb-out behavior, then we can start trying to identify the emotion that caused us to reach for it. We can go back to what we learned during our reality television research, and see if anything matches up, or feels like it's close to what we are going through. That gives us a great place to begin and will start to feel easier with time.

If you're still finding it difficult to connect with your emotions, we can try to stimulate them intentionally. Media like music, movies, or books can often evoke strong emotional responses—that's what makes them so powerful. Let's tap into that. Whenever I wanted to have a good cry, I used to watch reruns of the television show *Grey's Anatomy* or the film *Under the Tuscan Sun*. Those always helped trigger sadness and loss in me, serving as a surrogate when I couldn't release those emotions on my own. Spend some time finding media that triggers an emotional response in you and take note of what it is and what emotion you think it elicits.

IT FEELS TERRIBLE

The discomfort that comes with feeling your feelings isn't often talked about. Since our feelings can impede our work and cause us to shut down, we need to have some ways to manage them when they inevitably come up.

This is the part of healing that has been the most difficult for me. When I feel intense emotions, my first instinct is often to numb them out, and my go-to method of control has been turning to my phone. It's easy to distract myself, but that doesn't move me forward or help me heal. Instead, I try to acknowledge that I am feeling something intense, fight to try and identify it, and then let it happen. This can mean that I fall apart, ugly cry, or even scream, which is why I make sure I am in a safe place where I can do it. If I am not in a safe environment at that specific moment, I do my best to get to one quickly. That at least removes one deterrent to me experiencing my emotions.

One powerful fact that has always motivated me to sit with my emotions is the "ninety-second rule," a concept introduced by brain scientist Dr. Jill Bolte Taylor. Her research into our emotional responses reveals that when we react to something in our environment, a chemical process is triggered in the brain. This process, which involves the release of chemicals like noradrenaline, lasts for just ninety seconds. After that, any remaining emotional response is the result of our choice to stay in that emotional loop.

In other words, if we experience an upsetting thought, our body reacts by releasing the appropriate chemicals, causing us to feel emotions like anger. Within ninety seconds, those chemicals have been processed and flushed out of our system. If we continue to feel angry after that, it's because we are replaying the thought that triggered the emotion in the first place. This understanding keeps me fighting to sit with my feelings rather than running from them, knowing that they only last for ninety seconds, and what happens after that is up to me.

Once the ninety seconds are up, I assess whether there are actions I need to take. This could be communicating my feelings to someone, setting a boundary, or taking a step back to gain perspective. If action is necessary, I can approach it with a clearer mind, no longer fueled by the initial surge of emotion. If no action is needed, I remind myself that I have the power to let the feeling pass and return to a state of calm. Although I am far from perfect, this practice has helped me respond more thoughtfully to my emotions rather than being controlled by them.

IT'S NEVER PERFECT

What I've learned over time is that emotions require patience. They need space to come in, fulfill their purpose, and then naturally fade away. We don't need to overthink this; it's a natural process. As difficult as it is to accept, we can't control our emotions. They exist whether we want them to or not. The sooner we allow them to express what they need to, the sooner we can move forward with clarity and authenticity.

Understanding this has been a profound shift for me. Instead of resisting or trying to suppress my emotions, I've learned to approach them with curiosity and compassion. Each emotion, no matter how uncomfortable, carries valuable information about what we need, what we care about, and where we might be out of alignment in our lives. By sitting with our emotions, we give ourselves the chance to hear what they are telling us, to learn from them, and to respond in ways that are true to who we are.

This isn't about passively letting emotions run our lives. It's about actively engaging with them in a way that honors their role in our experience. Emotions are not the enemy. They are signals and guides that point us toward deeper understanding and healing. By giving them the space they need, we also give ourselves the space to grow.

And here's the truth: When we stop fighting our emotions and allow them to flow through us, we build emotional resilience. We learn that we can handle whatever comes our way and that no emotion is too big or too overwhelming. This is the path to emotional freedom: recognizing that our feelings, while intense, are temporary visitors, not permanent residents. They come and go, but we remain stronger and more self-aware with each passing wave.

"WHY DO I KEEP DOING THIS?" EXERCISE—*QUESTIONS TO IDENTIFY AND CHANGE THE URGE TO NUMB OUT*

1. What do you prefer to do when you feel uncomfortable emotions?
2. Do you have one favorite numb-out that you utilize? Does it change with different emotions or situations?

3. How were emotions expressed in your family growing up?
4. What emotions do you avoid the most? What benefit do you get by avoiding them, and how can you choose another way to experience these emotions?
5. What songs, movies, or other media help you feel something?
6. Is there a specific emotion you find yourself trying to trigger? Why do you think that is?
7. Pick your most frequent emotion and think about what message it might be trying to tell you.

CONTROL CHALLENGE

Next time you feel an uncomfortable emotion, **pause for three to five minutes** and just sit with it. **Don't try to numb out**—instead, notice where the emotion shows up in your body and what it feels like. Afterward, take a moment to reflect: How did it feel to just let it be?

Chapter 7

ANGER AND DISCOMFORT WITH STRONG EMOTIONS

When We Avoid Feelings That Are Out of Control

EMOTIONS THAT FEEL STRONG CAN BE DIFFERENT FOR EVERYONE. In many cases a person's level of fear or discomfort with a certain emotion makes the expression of it feel large. And as we've learned, our experiences growing up also impact our relationship with emotions. If we grew up feeling like certain emotions were only expressed in loud or intense ways, it can make those emotions feel stronger for us than for others who experienced them differently. Anger is one example that often comes to mind when thinking about strong emotions. It is also one that is commonly controlled and suppressed because of its intensity.

Anger is often misunderstood and dismissed as a destructive force that should be avoided or suppressed at all costs. But at its core, anger is a protective emotion. It's our internal warning system, coming to our aid when something in our environment threatens our well-being. Anger arises when we feel that a boundary has been crossed, when someone has hurt us, disrespected us, or violated our sense of fairness. It's an emotion that demands attention, pushing us to recognize that something is wrong, and that action is needed.

When we experience anger, it's as if a fire has been ignited within us, fueling our desire to defend ourselves or correct an injustice. Unlike emotions such as fear or sadness, which can leave us feeling helpless or vulnerable, anger empowers us. It sharpens our focus, gives us energy, and drives us to stand up for ourselves in ways we might not otherwise consider. In this sense, anger is not just an emotional reaction—it's a call to action, a signal that we need to assert our needs, protect our boundaries, and address the wrongs that have been done to us. In our fight, flight, freeze, and fawn response, anger is all fight.

FEAR OF FIRE

As far back as I can remember, I've always been deeply uncomfortable with anger. My mom often tells the story of how, even as a child, I would get distressed if my parents so much as raised their voices. They might not have been arguing, just having a normal discussion, but I would cover my ears and plead with them to stop fighting.

It would be easy to assume that my behavior stems from growing up in an abusive home, where anger was constant, dangerous, and caused harm to those I loved. But that couldn't be further from the truth. In reality, arguments were rare in my family. No one raised their voices, and keeping the peace was always the priority. On the surface, it might seem like growing up in a conflict-free environment is ideal. But like any extreme, it's not without its drawbacks. Because I was never around disagreements, I didn't know how to handle them healthily. I didn't realize that you could argue, work through the conflict, and then come back together. I grew up believing that a fight meant a relationship was doomed, and as a result, I avoided conflict at all costs.

By steering clear of any potential disagreement, I thought I was in control of my anger, believing I could simply avoid it whenever I chose. But the truth is, I wasn't controlling my anger—I was controlling myself to avoid feeling it. Anger felt wild and unpredictable, like a fire that could quickly get out of hand. My fear and lack of understanding of this emotion made it seem far scarier than it actually was. For most of my life, I let this fear dictate how I navigated conflicts and relationships, trying to suppress or sidestep anger rather than acknowledging and dealing with it. Just like Justine, a member of my community shared:

> *I struggle a lot with anger. If I'm angry with someone else I always hide it as it always feels out of control and I was brought up to believe it was a bad emotion and made you a nasty person. I would always stuff it down until it became way too much and either lashed out by kicking things or by self-harming (I never hit someone else). I always thought if I'm angry at myself then at least it's not directed toward anyone else. I even become angry at myself for being angry at someone else.*

The belief that anger is an uncontrollable emotion is incredibly common, and I think this stems from the fact that anger is often used to cover or suppress deeper, more vulnerable feelings. For example, instead of expressing hurt, which makes me feel exposed, I might convey anger because it feels more protective. The fear of exposing our more vulnerable emotions and not having our needs met can drive anger to feel more intense. When we are in a position of feeling vulnerable, we can easily feel out of control, and anger can be that protective cover. If we're operating from a fight-or-flight state, anger can feel unpredictable and scary because we're trying to simultaneously control everything beneath it.

Anger can also be a secondary reaction after we've been continuously pushed beyond our boundaries. For some of us, if we've been experiencing a hurtful situation and have been taught to suppress our emotions, eventually we'll be unable to keep enduring the hurt and our anger comes in to protect us. This is how my mom explained her experience with anger when I discussed this with her. She explained that anger felt out of control for her because it was the final straw. She had already gone through the hurt or pain, and when the harm continued, anger was the only response left. It wasn't the first emotion she felt, but rather the result of being pushed beyond her limits.

ANGER OUT

When we talk about anger, we often picture someone fighting, yelling, or lashing out—taking some action meant to hurt or intimidate another person. This perception is rooted in the fact that anger is frequently associated with outward, aggressive expressions. In many cultures, anger is seen as a powerful emotion that drives people to defend themselves or assert dominance, often through loud or forceful behavior. This makes it easy to equate anger with actions like shouting, slamming doors, or engaging in physical confrontations. These visible displays of anger are what society most commonly recognizes and responds to, reinforcing the idea that anger must be externalized to be acknowledged. This could lead us to believe that in order to get our anger out we have to express it through physical actions.

To assist with this idea of expressing anger outwardly in a controlled environment, in 2008 Japan opened its first "rage room," where people could go and smash things as a way of expressing their frustrations. This was done in the hope that, instead of taking out their anger on other people, people could hold on to those feelings and release them in a controlled environment—by smashing televisions, breaking furniture, and hurling objects against the walls. The idea behind the rage room is to provide a safe, cathartic outlet for pent-up anger, allowing individuals to physically vent their emotions without causing harm to others or damaging personal relationships.

However, the potential benefits of using a rage room are short-lived. While smashing objects might offer a temporary release of pent-up anger and provide an immediate sense of relief, it doesn't address the root of the problem. In therapeutic terms, a rage room is considered a "distraction-based coping skill." In a way it could be seen as another manifestation of control. It gives us a less destructive outlet for our anger than acting on our initial impulses, but it doesn't help us truly process or understand what we're feeling. By resorting to smashing and breaking things, we might inadvertently reinforce negative coping mechanisms, teaching ourselves that aggression is the only way to deal with frustration.

Instead, it's crucial to learn how to listen to our anger and decipher what it's trying to tell us. Anger often signals that something in our life needs attention or change. For example, if we get angry because we discover our significant other has cheated on us, the initial surge of anger is valid, and expressing it to trusted friends and family can be helpful. But the real work lies in taking constructive action within the relationship. This might involve having a difficult conversation with our partner, working to rebuild trust if we choose to continue the relationship, or deciding to end it and assert our need for respect and boundaries. By channeling our anger into thoughtful, intentional actions, we can create positive change rather than just temporarily blow off steam.

ANGER IN

External expression is just one facet of anger, and it's not the only way it manifests. The idea that anger must be expressed through outward aggression overlooks the many other ways people experience and deal with this emotion. For some, anger might simmer beneath the surface, leading to passive-aggressive behavior, withdrawal, or even self-directed harm. Just like this story I received from a member of my community:

> *It wasn't until I was twenty-seven and I shared in group therapy that I didn't get angry. Never raised my voice or lost my cool. The therapist listened and then pointed out the fact that I self-harmed. I didn't see her point, but she went on to say that self-harm was probably the angriest thing I could do. Her comment took me by surprise, and when I thought back the two things coincided. I stopped being angry the minute I started self-harming. My mind fluttered through all of the hospital visits and times I had totally lost control of my self-harming. I can now see from the outside just how angry and violent these acts were. Even now over ten years on it's still my go-to thought whenever I feel overwhelmed by an emotion, but at least I can sometimes stop and ask why am I angry now. Even if it doesn't always stop the act, it sometimes does, and that all started with realizing that anger isn't always shouting and screaming outwardly. Sometimes it's a silent moment of solitude with a "calm" slip of a blade. Because ironically that's the safe way to be angry in my world.*

Many of my patients often say, "If it's not hurting anyone else, why do I have to stop?" I understand this sentiment. For those of us who prioritize others over ourselves, it can seem like internalizing our anger is a good solution for everyone. We may also feel like our anger is too much or too big to express safely, so we turn it on ourselves instead of others. If we've done this most of our lives and haven't been taught other options, it may be the only way we know how to cope.

Turning anger inward can feel easier and safer. We don't have to involve anyone else in our upset and can maintain peace in our external relationships. By keeping our anger inside, we avoid the potential conflicts and discomfort that might arise from expressing it outwardly. This inward direction of anger can take many forms: self-criticism, rumination, withdrawal, or even self-sabotage. We might turn our anger inside by blaming ourselves for things that aren't our fault, replaying negative events in our minds, or isolating ourselves from others. While it might seem like we're protecting ourselves, we're actually creating more harm. Internalizing anger prevents us from addressing the issues that triggered it in the first place, leaving us stuck in a state of unresolved tension.

This can create a cycle of self-punishment where our anger festers and grows, leading to feelings of worthlessness, depression, or anxiety. We might believe we're avoiding making the situation worse; however, this avoidance often comes at a high personal cost. The unexpressed anger doesn't disappear—it can build up inside us, leading to physical symptoms like headaches, stomach issues, or high blood pressure. Over time, this suppressed anger can erode our self-esteem, making us feel powerless and disconnected from our true feelings.

ANGER OR ASSERTION

Understanding the nuances of anger is crucial to harnessing its potential as a positive force rather than letting it pull us under. Anger, at its core, is a response to perceived threats or injustices, and it serves as a signal that something needs to be addressed. The challenge lies in distinguishing between anger and assertion.

Anger often comes with a burst of intense emotion, which can sometimes lead to impulsive and reactive behavior. This is the danger of anger: Without mindfulness, it can drive us to act out in ways that are destructive or counterproductive. We might lash out, say things we don't mean, or create conflict where none is needed. This impulsive reaction can obscure the true message of our anger and derail our efforts to resolve the issue constructively.

When I was in my early twenties I engaged in a lot of rage-filled behaviors. I know this makes me look bad, but I used to go out with my friends and pick fights with my boyfriend at the time or some unsuspecting person at the bar. It was bad and I am embarrassed to even admit I acted like that. After getting back into therapy I realized that it was because my dad was really sick. He was in and out of the hospital and I was going to graduate school full-time while also working two jobs. I was numbing out, trying to control my circumstances by staying busy and stuffing down my anger at what felt like the unfairness of life. When things slowed down and I was out drinking with friends, I wasn't able to keep the barrier up. My anger came rushing out on anyone and everyone around me. It was messy, hurtful, and impulsive.

Assertion, on the other hand, is the art of channeling anger into purposeful, clear, and respectful communication. It involves taking the underlying message of our anger—the sense that something is wrong or that our boundaries have been crossed—and expressing it in a way that is constructive and focused. Assertiveness means addressing the issue head-on without aggression or hostility, but rather with clarity and respect. It's about standing up for ourselves in a way that seeks to resolve the situation rather than escalate it.

Being assertive has always seemed like a delicate concept to me. I used to believe that speaking up, asking for what I wanted, or saying no could be hurtful or even provoke conflict. However, I've learned that addressing issues directly and openly is far better than agreeing to something and harboring resentment later. For instance, just a few weeks ago, someone asked if I could speak at their daughter's school. In the past, I might have reluctantly agreed, even if it wasn't convenient for me, out of fear of causing upset or tension. This time I asked about the budget and time commitment and took time to decide if it fit my schedule. I decided it wouldn't and told them that, unfortunately, I wasn't available. Even though I felt guilty for a second, that feeling was quickly replaced with pride. I had asserted myself and it felt good.

The key difference between anger and assertion is control and intention. While anger is a natural, raw response to a situation, assertion is a mindful choice to use that emotion to advocate for ourselves in a way that promotes understanding and resolution. It's about transforming the energy of anger into a tool for effective communication and positive change. By listening to the messages our anger conveys and responding with intention rather than reactivity, we can move forward constructively and ensure that our anger serves as a catalyst for personal growth and healthier relationships.

LISTENING TO OUR ANGER

It's important to find a healthy way to express all that we feel without lashing out or stuffing it down. That's the key: learning to acknowledge and listen to our anger without allowing it to consume us. It's about striking a balance between honoring our emotions and responding to them in a way that promotes growth rather than harm. This means developing the ability to sit with our anger, understanding what it's trying to tell us, and then expressing it in a way that's both constructive and compassionate. By doing so, we can use our anger as a tool for positive change rather than letting it dictate our actions or undermine our well-being.

When we are uncomfortable with strong emotions like anger, we can struggle to hear the messages it sends, often assuming that we're overreacting or that our feelings aren't valid. Like I said before, anger is a powerful indicator that something in our life needs attention. I have always believed that's why it's so loud and can feel aggressive. It's our alarm system, telling us when something is off or a situation is out of balance. By listening to our anger, we can gain valuable insights into what's really bothering us and where changes are necessary. If we don't listen to it, we will keep getting the same results in our life, even if those things are upsetting us.

Instead of dismissing or suppressing our anger, we can use it as a guide to help us identify where we may need to reassess our life choices or even our relationships. Anger can reveal when we feel disrespected, unheard, or taken advantage of, prompting us to take action to protect ourselves. It can also highlight areas of our lives that no longer align with our values or goals, pushing us to make necessary changes. In this way, anger isn't just a negative emotion—it's a catalyst for growth and self-advocacy, helping us navigate our lives with greater clarity and purpose. So, take a beat before reacting and consider what your anger is trying to tell you. What is it trying to protect you from? If we take that into consideration, we can decide when and where to take action. This allows us to respect our anger, get to know it even, and act on it when appropriate.

WE ALL NEED PROTECTION

For most of my life, I've believed that certain behaviors could only be justified by anger. Placing a boundary or speaking up for myself didn't feel acceptable unless I was upset, as if acting out of spite somehow made my stern response more valid. It was a way to convince myself that I wasn't being mean or rude but rather that my need for personal space or mutual respect was a response to something far worse. This revelation is new to me, and I have to admit, I'm embarrassed by it. It's unsettling to realize that I've felt incapable of standing up for myself or simply saying no without the crutch of anger. Instead, I've resorted to reacting out of frustration, as if that were the only way to justify my needs.

This urge to use anger as a shield has extended beyond assertive behaviors, seeping into my ability to do things for myself. When I want to take time for myself or indulge in something I love, I struggle to justify it unless it's driven by some form of upset. It's as if joy alone isn't enough, and the only way I can prioritize myself is if I'm fueled by anger or frustration. I'm beginning to see how damaging this mindset is, how it traps me in a cycle where self-care and personal joy are only permissible if they're a reaction to something negative.

However, I've also come to realize that anger itself isn't inherently harmful—it's how we respond to it that matters. The power of anger lies not just in its intensity but in its ability to illuminate what we need to address. When we listen to what our anger is telling us without letting it consume us, we can use it as a tool for positive change. It helps us identify what needs to be confronted and gives us the courage to do so. Anger can remind us that we have the right to stand up for ourselves, to demand respect, and to protect our well-being. In this way, anger isn't our enemy—it's a powerful ally that, when understood and channeled effectively, can help us navigate life's complexities with strength and integrity.

By recognizing this dual nature of anger, I'm slowly learning to shift away from the need to justify my actions through it and toward understanding that my needs and desires are valid on their own. The challenge now is to embrace them with the same conviction that anger once provided but from a place of self-compassion and balance. And if I'm being honest, it's difficult, and I haven't quite figured it out yet.

GETTING TO KNOW OUR ANGER

When we are uncomfortable with a specific emotion it can be hard for us to get to know it. Even engaging with it can feel dangerous, which is why we often don't know anything about our strong emotions. It's like that bully at school we avoided like the plague; we didn't know anything about them either. It was better and safer for us to keep our distance. However, in the case of our anger, we must learn about it and understand its role in our lives so we can understand the message it's sending. The easiest way to do this is to understand our triggers. Think back to the last time you felt anger—whether it was directed inward or outward. What had happened that day? Who did you interact with? If you can recall, what was your thought process like?

Taking the time to consider what led up to an angry response can show us where our weak spots are. I don't mean "weak" in a judgmental sense, but rather as an indicator of where we are most susceptible to the emotions that trigger our anger. By identifying these vulnerabilities, we can begin to understand what our anger is trying to protect us from. For example, if we think back on the last time we got really angry and if it was during a conversation where we felt dismissed or unheard, that anger might be signaling a deeper fear of being insignificant or unimportant. If we try and remember what thoughts were going on in our head during that time, we may find we had self-deprecating ones like "I am never good enough" or "I should just keep my mouth shut, no one cares what I have to say anyway." While doing this kind of digging can be difficult and sometimes painful, it helps us better understand our anger and the role it plays in our lives.

Next, we should look for patterns. Do we usually get angry at home, at work, or with a specific person in our life? As a therapist, much of my work involves identifying these patterns. It's normal to have occasional outbursts, but if the same situations or people consistently trigger our anger, there may be something deeper going on. By recognizing these patterns, we gain a better understanding of how to manage our response. Remember, anger isn't a bad emotion—it just needs to be acknowledged and addressed.

AIMING AT THE WRONG TARGET

Misplaced anger is crucial to address because it often manifests in ways that don't directly relate to the actual source of our frustration. For instance, you might find yourself snapping at your spouse over something trivial, like them leaving a dish in the sink or forgetting to pick up groceries. On the surface, these incidents seem minor and may not connect to any deep-seated fear or belief about yourself—they might just be annoying. However, this kind of anger can often indicate that we're controlling our emotions in one situation and then releasing them in a safer environment, such as with someone we trust or feel comfortable around.

For example, you might be experiencing stress at work due to an overbearing boss, unrealistic deadlines, or feeling unappreciated. However, instead of addressing these issues directly—perhaps because of fear of confrontation or job security—you might suppress your frustration. Later, when you're at home, this pent-up anger could spill over into interactions with your family, leading to arguments over seemingly insignificant issues. Another scenario could be dealing with a challenging friendship where you feel taken advantage of but are hesitant to speak up. The unexpressed resentment might later emerge as irritability toward your partner or even your children.

If you notice that you repeatedly get angry with certain people but struggle to identify a significant reason or trigger, it could be a sign that your anger is being redirected from where it truly belongs. Recognizing this pattern is essential because it allows you to address the real source of your frustration, whether it's setting boundaries at work, having difficult conversations in your friendships, or acknowledging deeper feelings of stress or insecurity. By doing so, you can prevent unnecessary conflict in your relationships and create a more harmonious environment both at home and within yourself. Additionally, it helps ensure that your anger is expressed in a way that is both constructive and appropriate to the situation, rather than causing harm to those who may not be the true source of your upset.

BUILDING RESILIENCE

Resilience is our ability to weather the ups and downs of life and keep our cool. It is important to consider the impact of resilience when discussing intense emotions like anger. If our resilience is low we can find ourselves flying off the handle over minor inconveniences, feeling overwhelmed easily, and struggling to keep up with our life. If we have taken the time to build up our resilience, we can better handle the stress of running late to work, manage that conflict with our coworkers with ease, and stay focused. Our ability to ride the waves of life without getting pulled under is invaluable to managing strong emotions.

The good news is that building resilience is relatively simple, but it does require consistency. For example, when I don't get a good night's sleep, I become easily agitated, quick to anger and lose my patience. My lack of proper rest directly impacts my resilience the next day, making it harder to handle stress. This shows how essential self-care practices, like getting enough sleep, are in maintaining our resilience. You can find thousands of lists all touting complex ways to build up your resilience or engage in proper self-care. I am here to tell you that the simpler it is, the better.

Meaning that in order to build sustainable resilience we need to stick to the basics and do them consistently.

Whenever I talk about resilience-building, I use the acronym HALT. It stands for "hungry, angry, lonely, and tired." It's a tool utilized frequently in Alcoholics Anonymous to support those in recovery to think clearly and make good choices. When we are too hungry or tired, we aren't clearheaded and can make impulsive decisions that aren't in line with our values or goals. If we are already angry or lonely, it's going to be hard for us not to let that color our reactions to other areas in our lives. In short, checking in on these four items, and making a point to prioritize their wellness, will ensure we are better prepared to manage life's ups and downs.

Two other important resilience-building tools I like to add to the list are showering regularly and taking care of any illness we have. These are simple things, but they can be vital to our resilience. Just the other day I was feeling really lonely. I recently moved to a new state and I don't have many friends here. I was allowing myself to ruminate on this fact, feeling sad, alone, and hopeless. After feeling this way for about an hour I decided I needed to take a shower and reboot my brain. It sounds silly, but sometimes a shower can change your life. It can be like a hard reset and give you the space needed to get out of a funk.

Having a cold or chronic illness can also lower our resilience. When we are physically down and out it's going to be hard for us to muster up the strength not to let anger or another strong emotion run and possibly ruin the show. If we can find little ways to improve our health or manage symptoms, it will help put us in a better position to navigate our emotional reactions in a constructive way.

Being able to focus on these key areas of our life to help manage our core needs will set us up for success in managing our strong emotions. It will also help us avoid other more destructive options like indulging in substances to cope. Alcohol and drugs may provide a momentary escape, but they ultimately undermine our resilience by interfering with our natural coping mechanisms. These substances can dull our emotions, making it harder to process and address the underlying issues that are causing us stress. We end up suppressing our emotions, which can lead to increased anxiety, depression, and a reduced ability to handle future challenges. Learning to manage stress through mindfulness, exercise, connecting with others, or seeking support from a therapist or counselor can help us build the skills necessary for long-term resilience.

DEALING WITH IT

Understanding the message our anger is sending is valuable, but knowing how to incorporate that insight into our lives can be challenging. This is where I often struggle. I can fully grasp a concept, but I'm not always sure how to apply it in practice. It's like reading all about how to jump rope, but when I step up to the rope swinging in the air, I can't quite figure out how to jump in. However, jumping in and trying is where we learn and change, even if we step on the rope a few times first. If we can take the first jump to try and engage with our anger differently, we can work toward seeing it as a helpful tool and resource, instead of something to be feared and ignored.

The one thing that consistently helps me avoid acting out in anger is taking a break. I need to give myself some space between the situation or trigger and my response. Taking a moment to pause and breathe can save me from falling back into old habits and give me the chance to make a positive change instead. This break allows me to approach the situation with a clearer mind, making it easier to implement what I've learned. Sometimes this means I will step away from a conversation for a minute, pop into the bathroom and breathe, or even just verbally let them know that I need a minute to think. Being able to initiate a break has saved me from so many unnecessary fights that aren't in alignment with who I want to be.

We all know how important clear communication is in all areas of our life. However, as a recovering people-pleaser who is terrified of conflict, communicating about intense emotions is at the bottom of my list of things I want to do. In learning to add a break between my emotions and my reaction, I have found a simple therapeutic tool that can defuse potential upsets while allowing me to speak up about something that is making me angry.

Those who have experienced couples counseling may be aware of the use of "I statements." While these may have been overused in this setting, they can be an effective way to communicate our feelings to others. It helps to shift the conversation from focusing on the blame to instead focusing on how it makes us feel. For example, instead of telling my mom that I hate it when she shares my personal information with the whole family, and yelling about how embarrassing and disrespectful she is, I can focus my comments on how it affects me, saying, "I feel hurt and embarrassed when my personal information is shared without my permission." This approach helps me communicate my emotions more effectively and also encourages a more constructive and empathetic dialogue. It allows the other person to understand the impact of their actions without feeling attacked, making it more likely that they'll respond positively.

Using "I statements" does take practice. However, if you give yourself the space to think before speaking, focusing on how you feel and how the situation has affected you, it can make your communication more honest and sincere. This approach helps ensure that your message is clear and centered on your personal experience, rather than placing blame on others.

Another tool that can be helpful after adding a break is "opposite action." When I am really angry about something and want to isolate and talk negatively about myself, I do the opposite. I reach out, connect with those around me, and look for ways I can lift myself up. This technique takes more determination up front, but the relief I feel is almost immediate. Just the other day I had gotten into an argument with my husband, Sean. My default response is to retreat, not talk about it, and hope that my silence sends a message—essentially, trying to control the situation. But I've learned that this never serves me or my relationships. So instead of controlling the silence, I went over to Sean, apologized for my part in the argument, and hugged him. I felt better right away, and this disagreement didn't drag on for days. Instead, it was remedied in less than an hour. If you can push against that initial urge to act like you always do, this can be a game changer.

Accepting anger as a part of our emotional landscape is a journey that requires patience and persistence. It's important to recognize that working through our anger is not a one-time fix but an ongoing process. Anger will inevitably be a part of our lives, and its presence is not something to be eradicated, but understood and managed. By exploring how anger serves us and influences our relationships, we can cultivate a deeper respect for this powerful emotion.

Understanding anger's role enables us to collaborate with it rather than resist it, leading to more meaningful and constructive outcomes. Remember, each step you take toward embracing and managing your anger is a step toward greater self-awareness and personal growth. With time, commitment, and compassion, you can transform your relationship with anger into a source of strength and empowerment, guiding you toward a more balanced and fulfilling life.

MORE THAN ANGER

I would be remiss if I didn't acknowledge that anger isn't the only emotion we tend to shy away from. I've used it throughout this chapter as an example that is easily accessible to me, but the same concept can apply to any strong emotion we feel. While anger has been my default emotion for protection, others may find joy, sadness, or fear as their strongest emotion. The concepts and tools can still be applied. Our ability to be open to our experiences and understand what drives them will help us to approach our strong emotions with grace and acceptance rather than shame. We can learn to work with these emotions, using them as a guide to uncover areas of our lives we've been neglecting and redirect our focus to where it's needed most.

For some of us, positive emotions like joy, excitement, and even elation can feel just as intimidating as anger. This can be especially true if we're not accustomed to experiencing them or allowing ourselves to. If all we've known is hurt, disappointment, or constant stress, feeling positive emotions can make us feel exposed or vulnerable too. It's as if embracing happiness or excitement leaves us unguarded, fearing that the joy might be fleeting or that something bad might follow. In a way, avoiding these positive emotions becomes a form of self-preservation, a way to protect ourselves from potential disappointment or loss.

This avoidance can be just as damaging as suppressing anger. By shutting ourselves off from joy and excitement, we limit our ability to fully experience life's richness. We may think we're protecting ourselves, but in reality, we're depriving ourselves of the happiness and fulfillment that these emotions bring. It's important to recognize that feeling joy doesn't make us weak—it makes us human. Allowing ourselves to embrace positive emotions is an essential part of living a balanced, healthy life. Just as we need to learn to listen to our anger, we also need to allow ourselves to experience and enjoy the full spectrum of emotions, knowing that it's okay to be happy, excited, and even elated. These emotions are not just fleeting moments of pleasure; they are vital aspects of our well-being that remind us of our capacity for love, connection, and growth.

"WHY DO I KEEP DOING THIS?" EXERCISE— *QUESTIONS TO BETTER UNDERSTAND AND ENGAGE WITH OUR ANGER*

1. How were strong emotions dealt with as you were growing up? How did your parents/guardians express them to you in your home?
2. If anger is a primary emotion for you, when do you find yourself feeling most angry? What people or situations bring out this feeling most often?
3. What underlying emotions drive your anger response most?
4. How do you express your anger or other strong emotions? Are these emotions expressed mostly inward or outward?
5. What emotions have impacted your relationships most? If you implemented one of the tools within this chapter into your life, how would it change your relationships?
6. What is your experience with positive emotions like joy and excitement? How often do you allow yourself to feel these, and where can you look for areas to allow more joy into your life?

CONTROL CHALLENGE

For the next week, set aside **five to ten minutes daily** to check in with your emotions using this simple practice:

Name it: Identify the strongest emotion you've felt that day (anger, joy, frustration, excitement, sadness, etc.).

Feel it: Take a moment to sit with that emotion. Where do you feel it in your body? What thoughts come up?

Express it differently: If you tend to suppress emotions, try expressing them outwardly (journaling, movement, conversation). If you tend to react outwardly, practice a pause before responding.

Balance with joy: Each day, intentionally seek or create one small moment of joy—whether through music, movement, connection, or something that makes you laugh.

Reflect: At the end of the week, ask yourself: "How did this practice impact my emotional awareness, relationships, and resilience?"

Chapter 8

PUFFER FISHING AND PROTECTING OURSELVES

Why We Push People Away

Protecting ourselves is something we're hardwired to do. It's a primal instinct, deeply rooted in our biology. If we find ourselves in a dark alley and a stranger suddenly rushes toward us, our immediate response is to run or defend ourselves to survive. We might pull out our pepper spray, scream for help, or do whatever it takes to keep ourselves safe. This instinct isn't something we consciously decide; it's an automatic reaction, a vital part of our survival toolkit.

This protective instinct doesn't just kick in when our physical safety is threatened. It also emerges when our emotional well-being feels at risk. Just as we'd shield our bodies from harm, we instinctively protect our hearts and minds from pain, criticism, and rejection. Control in this case manifests as putting up walls, deflecting uncomfortable truths, and even pushing people away—all to protect ourselves from feeling hurt or vulnerable.

Our urge to protect our emotional selves is natural and can be helpful to keep us safe in situations that could truly be harmful. But if we find ourselves relying on this form of protection too often, it can get in the way of cultivating genuine connection with those around us. When we're too focused on shielding ourselves from potential pain or criticism, we close ourselves off from others. This makes it difficult to form deep and meaningful relationships. Our defenses become barriers, keeping people at arm's length. This distance prevents us from experiencing true intimacy and understanding within our relationships.

I've always been my harshest critic, constantly striving for perfection and tearing myself down when I fall short. This relentless drive has fueled my success, making me a Type A overachiever. It also means that I'm hypersensitive to any form of feedback. I could hear nine glowing compliments about a presentation I gave, but if there's even one critique, it overshadows everything else. Suddenly, the entire effort feels like a failure.

This sensitivity isn't just about wanting to do well, it's about tying my worth to my performance. When someone points out a flaw, it's not just the presentation that's under scrutiny; it feels like I am. This is where defensiveness creeps in, pushing me to protect myself from the sting of criticism, even if it means shutting down or rejecting the feedback entirely. It's a reflex, an attempt to preserve my sense of self-worth by deflecting anything that threatens it.

This behavior doesn't just affect my self-esteem; it interferes with my relationships too. When you combine this defensive response with my aversion to conflict, it's no surprise that I used to have a habit of ending relationships quickly. Rather than face uncomfortable conversations or allow someone to point out areas where I might need to grow, I'd shut down or walk away. It felt easier to cut ties than to stay and risk feeling exposed, criticized, or vulnerable. But in doing so, I was also cutting myself off from the potential for deeper connections and personal growth.

PUFFER FISHING

At my recent fortieth birthday party, one of my closest friends gave a toast that caught me completely off guard. She raised her glass and said, "I'd like to congratulate us all for making it here because, you know Kati, if she doesn't like you, she'll cut you off quick." Everyone laughed and clinked their glasses, but I was left stunned. Was that really how people saw me? Did I truly cut people off quickly, without a second thought or any warning?

At that moment, it hit me; this wasn't just a joke, it was a reflection of a pattern I hadn't fully recognized in myself. The laughter around me was lighthearted, but the truth behind her words landed heavily. Had my defensiveness and aversion to conflict turned me into someone who dismissed people too easily, severing ties before they could challenge me or get too close? The realization was unsettling. I knew this had affected my romantic relationships in the past, but I thought my friendships were different. I thought I had gotten better. I was wrong.

My first realization of this type of behavior was over fifteen years ago. I was sitting in my therapist's office, explaining why I needed to break up with my boyfriend. I told her he didn't challenge me, that I felt like I was doing all the giving, and that I just didn't want to be with him anymore. She asked if I had brought up any of my concerns with him. Of course I hadn't, and she encouraged me to talk it out before making any decisions. By our next session, I had already ended the relationship and was confidently listing all the reasons why it was the right choice.

That's when she stopped me and said, "Kati, you're a puffer fish."

"A what?" I asked, genuinely puzzled.

"A puffer fish," she explained. "You're soft and sensitive on the inside, but whenever someone gets too close, you stick out your spines to protect yourself and keep them at a distance. You just puffer-fished your last boyfriend."

While the name itself is funny, the realization was anything but. What she said felt like a mirror I wasn't ready to look into. I had been so focused on protecting myself that I hadn't realized how often I pushed people away, especially when they got too close to my vulnerabilities. The puffer fish metaphor stuck with me, a reminder that my defensiveness wasn't just a quirk, it was a barrier that kept me from truly connecting with others. To find out that this was still affecting my relationships today was a wake-up call. I had to get a handle on my intense need to protect myself. I had to learn how to let people in, weather upsets, and be vulnerable. Ugh.

TOXIC INDEPENDENCE

Keeping people at arm's length can feel safe for many reasons. If we don't let people get close, they can't hurt us. In my case, if I don't count on someone to do something, then I won't be let down when they don't do it. Growing up, I always preferred to do my own work, hated group projects, and took pride in my independence. As I got older, I realized that my need for independence was negatively impacting my relationships. I was caught in an unhealthy cycle where I wouldn't ask for help because I wanted to do it all myself, I'd get stressed out because it was too much for one person to do, and then I'd resent those around me for not helping. It was total control chaos. I was angry and let down all the time when that was exactly what I was trying to avoid. My incessant need for independence had turned toxic.

This cycle wasn't just exhausting; it was isolating. The more I tried to do everything on my own, the more I distanced myself from the people who cared about me. I'd silently suffer under the weight of my responsibilities, telling myself that it was better this way, that at least I wouldn't have to depend on anyone and risk being let down. But in reality, I was setting myself up for disappointment. I'd feel overwhelmed and unsupported, even though I was the one pushing others away. It became a vicious loop: The more I refused to ask for help, the more I needed it, and the angrier I became when I didn't receive it, despite never asking in the first place.

Toxic independence almost acts just like an autoimmune disorder—meant to protect us, but in reality it ends up attacking us from within. Just as an immune system mistakenly targets healthy cells, our drive to do everything on our own starts to erode our well-being and relationships. What begins as a strategy for self-preservation turns into a source of stress, isolation, and resentment. This leaves us more vulnerable than if we had simply allowed ourselves to lean on others when needed.

My way of defending against pain was causing more of it, and it became clear that my need for control and self-sufficiency was creating its own set of problems.

BEING DEFENSIVE

This defense mechanism extended into how I handled feedback and criticism. I've always had a strong aversion to the phrase "constructive criticism," because, to me, it never feels constructive. When someone gives me negative feedback, it's as if my ears shut off, and one of two things happen. Either my self-deprecating thoughts kick into overdrive, drowning out their voice, or I start to discredit them in my mind, so I don't have to take their words to heart.

I know this reaction holds me back, stunting my growth and keeping me from improving. It's hard to listen to someone else point out your flaws when you're already painfully aware of them. It feels like they're just adding fuel to a fire that's already burning too hot. This defensiveness is a shield, protecting me from the sting of criticism, but it's also a barrier—one that keeps me from embracing the very feedback that could help me become better by controlling how I absorb it.

Luckily, I'm not alone in my urge to put up barriers and protect myself from hurtful feedback. Defense mechanisms are numerous and incredibly common. They are our mind's way of shielding us from emotional pain and discomfort. These mechanisms often operate without us even realizing it, kicking in automatically to help us cope with situations that feel threatening or overwhelming.

We develop these defenses as a means of self-preservation. Whether it's deflecting criticism, avoiding difficult emotions, or distancing ourselves from others, these strategies are designed to protect our sense of self. Understanding these defense mechanisms is crucial because once we recognize them, we can begin to see how they shape our interactions and responses. To help you better acknowledge the defense mechanisms you might rely on most, let's explore the fourteen most common ones. I know that sounds like a lot, but each plays a unique role and serves a different purpose.

OVERTHINKING IT

Let's start with the one I lean on most: intellectualization, or overthinking. To intellectualize is to take all emotion out of an experience and look at it in a cold, logical, and almost research-like way. I blame my education, but I know I do this to avoid feeling uncomfortable emotions while still being able to talk about them with people in my life. It's like I can describe to you what my emotions are, but I don't allow myself to feel them. A member of my community said it best when she shared:

> *After my last relationship ended, I threw myself into researching relationship dynamics. I took countless relationship workshops and read all the books I could find online. I spent hours reading articles about attachment styles and dissecting every conversation I had had with him, trying to pinpoint exactly where things went wrong. Now, a year later I realize that I never actually grieved the loss of the relationship, I just learned about it. I don't know why I keep doing this, but I know it's not helping.*

RATIONALIZATION

Rationalization is another favorite defense mechanism of mine because it ties nicely into intellectualization. Instead of admitting that we are feeling upset or disappointed that we didn't get that promotion, we say that it's better this way because we don't need the extra stress. We can do this to let ourselves down easily or explain away someone's hurtful behavior. We sidestep the real cause of our feelings and instead focus on another more rational explanation.

STUFFING IT DOWN

Another common defense mechanism is repression, where we push away unhappy thoughts or feelings so they don't reach our conscious mind. This often happens when we repress memories of past pain or abuse. We might convince ourselves that these events never happened. When those emotions start to surface, we quickly distract ourselves to avoid acknowledging them.

For me, repression shows up in physical ways. This could be difficulty sleeping, tension in my neck and shoulders, and an underlying sense of unease that I can't quite place. It's as if my body is carrying the weight of the emotions I refuse to confront, and over time, this unresolved tension can even make me sick.

DENIAL

Similar to repression, denial is another defense mechanism we use to stuff things down. Instead of pushing uncomfortable thoughts or feelings out of our awareness, we refuse to acknowledge the truth of what's happening and may even deny that it's occurring at all. I have seen this a lot in people struggling with addiction, downplaying how often they drink or use drugs. It can also happen to any of us who aren't ready or able to acknowledge what's really going on in our lives. Here's a recent example I received from a member of my community:

> "*When I was a kid, I learned pretty quickly that showing emotions, especially the tough ones like anger or sadness, didn't go over well with my parents. They weren't harsh, but they definitely had high expectations. So when I felt disappointed, hurt, or even scared, I figured the best way to deal with it was to just push those feelings down. If I didn't acknowledge them, then maybe they'd go away—and, more importantly, I wouldn't disappoint my parents by not being the "good" kid they expected me to be.*
>
> *One time, in third grade, I brought home a report card with a B in math. My dad didn't say much, but I could see the hint of disappointment in his eyes. That look was enough for me to decide then and there that I would never let him see me as anything less than perfect. So instead of admitting how upset I was, I shoved that feeling deep down and focused on how I could avoid that happening again. It became a pattern. I'd get a bad grade, mess up in sports, or have a fight with a friend, and instead of letting myself feel sad or frustrated, I'd bury it. I convinced myself that as long as I didn't feel it, it wasn't real.*

But the emotions never really went away. They'd come out in other ways, like the tension headaches I started getting in high school or the insomnia that hit when I couldn't stop obsessing over whether I'd let someone down. It was like my body was carrying around all this unspoken disappointment and fear, but I had no idea how to deal with it. Even now, I catch myself doing it—pushing down those uncomfortable feelings because it feels easier than facing them.

REGRESSION

Regression is in many ways connected to repression. Not only because they sound alike, but because they can also work together like a tag team. When we stuff everything down or repress it for years, it can impede our emotional development. This can mean that when pushed to our limits or stressed by an event in our life, we can regress to a child version of ourselves. We can name-call, start sucking our thumb, or even throw a tantrum. Essentially, this defense mechanism pulls us back into a younger version of ourselves as a way of protecting us from the current pain.

I experienced this defense mechanism throughout college. I went away for school, which meant that I only came home for winter break and summer, spending most of my time on campus each year. However, whenever I returned to the house I grew up in, I found myself acting just like I did as a teenager. I would fight with my parents, be annoyed at them for wanting me to do chores around the house, and revert to the same defensive behaviors I thought I'd outgrown.

It was like stepping into that old environment brought me right back to the person I was when I last lived there. It was jarring and embarrassing, and I fought it each time I went home until I moved out on my own for good.

THIS DOESN'T BELONG HERE

Have you ever been really pissed off about something at work, and then you come home and take out your frustrations on your partner or spouse? That experience is called "displacement," and if we are honest, we have all done it at one time or another. We feel upset about something one person did and we take it out on someone else. I have always believed that this defense mechanism occurs because we don't always feel safe to express our feelings. In this example, we can't just tell our boss that they pissed us off. Instead, we hold on to it until it's safe to let it out, and that usually happens around people we love and know well.

PROJECTION

Another defense mechanism that involves inappropriately shifting blame is projection. Projection is when we take our difficult emotions or challenging qualities and place them onto someone else. For example, if we are angry with someone we can yell at them to stop being angry with us. We project onto them the emotion we are truly feeling. Doing this prevents us from having to claim and process our own emotional experience, and instead blame someone else for having it.

This phenomenon occurs frequently in therapy, where our therapist challenges us to acknowledge our true feelings and confront the parts of ourselves we may not like. Because we're not used to facing these emotions—or we're afraid of what they might reveal—it's common to push them onto our therapist in an effort to protect our current sense of self.

ADDRESSING IT INDIRECTLY

One way that I cope with feeling hurt or taken advantage of is to not say anything directly. I am being serious. Conflict is not something I walk right into; in fact, I try to avoid it at all costs. However, that doesn't mean I don't get mad or want to lash out. Instead of communicating directly, I use my other favorite defense mechanism: passive-aggressive behavior. I am not proud of it, but avoiding direct communication and trying to passively get someone to see my upset feels easier sometimes. This can mean that I sulk, withdraw, or use the silent treatment as a way of eliciting a response. I am hoping that the other person will reach out and ask what's wrong instead of having to start the difficult conversation myself.

While every one of these defense mechanisms is popular, this one could be the most common. We've all been in situations where we're upset but, for one reason or another, don't feel like we can openly express it. Other examples of passive-aggressive behavior are being sarcastic, purposefully being late, intentionally doing a task poorly, giving backhanded compliments, and, when asked if we are okay, denying anything is wrong and saying we're "fine."

ACTING OUT

When all of our passive-aggressive behaviors don't get us what we need, we can sometimes find ourselves acting out. Acting out is a defense mechanism that happens when we struggle to express our feelings in words, so instead we act on those emotions in ways that can be hurtful or damaging to ourselves or others. It's like our emotions are bubbling up inside us, and without a healthy outlet, they explode in ways that we might not even fully understand.

For example, let's say you're frustrated because your spouse or roommate hasn't been keeping up with their share of the housework. Instead of sitting down and having a direct conversation about it, you find yourself snapping at them over small things or giving them the cold shoulder all day. You might close doors a little harder than usual or sigh loudly when you pass by the dishes they didn't wash. These actions are ways of "acting out" your anger because, for whatever reason, you can't or don't want to express it directly. It's easy to see how this often overlaps with passive-aggressive behavior, and why they are frequently used together.

LAUGHING IT OFF

To lighten the mood, because those last two were doozies, let's talk about humor as a defense mechanism. We all know we do it. We make jokes about a situation or feeling to distract ourselves and others from it. The more uncomfortable we get, the more jokes we feel we need to tell. It's as if laughter can somehow shield us from the seriousness of what we're facing.

Humor can be a great way to cope with difficult emotions, but it can also be a way to avoid dealing with them. By turning everything into a joke, we might be deflecting our discomfort or minimizing the significance of what we're going through. It's important to recognize when we're using humor to genuinely connect with others and when we're using it to keep our true feelings at arm's length.

DISSOCIATION

When the situation we are faced with is too intense for us to manage, we may not be able to utilize any of the other defense mechanisms and we can dissociate. I like to think of dissociation as our brain pulling the rip cord on reality. It pulls us out and away from our current experience so that we don't feel as overwhelmed by it. It can seem like we leave our bodies or environment and create just enough distance to not feel as directly affected.

When this happens it often feels like we just spaced out or lost some time in our day. We could feel pulled into a daydream-like state or even like we are in a fog. Everyone experiences dissociation differently, but it's important to know that approximately half of all adults have experienced at least one dissociative episode. I have found myself losing time and dissociating during intense arguments or times of acute stress. I just kind of go through the motions, and afterward, I am unable to remember much of what happened. It can be scary, but it is a natural way that our brain tries to protect us, and it often happens when we don't have another way of dealing with the situation.

DISTORTION

Defense mechanisms can sometimes feel like they are using our brains against us, and that's definitely the case with distortion. This is when we change the facts so that we don't have to admit we feel upset or uncomfortable. In many ways, I've thought that distortion is similar to gaslighting, except we're doing it to ourselves—manipulating our perception of reality to avoid confronting our feelings. We can shift blame onto someone else or twist the situation so that we come out looking like the victim.

This can feel like it protects us from the parts of ourselves we don't like. If we already have low self-esteem, distortion can seem like a lifeline, helping us stay afloat by deflecting any responsibility for what's gone wrong. For example, if we get a bad review from our boss, we might convince ourselves that it's because they have it out for us, or that another team member didn't do their job, rather than facing the possibility that our performance could improve.

Distortion is particularly common among those with narcissistic personality disorder, as it often serves to deflect blame and preserve a fragile sense of self-worth. By altering our perception of reality, we protect ourselves from the discomfort of self-reflection, but in doing so, we also prevent ourselves from growing and learning from our mistakes.

REACTION FORMATION

For those of us who didn't feel safe or comfortable expressing our true feelings, reaction formation often becomes our go-to defense mechanism. I think of this as the "fake it till you make it" strategy, where instead of admitting we're hurt or feeling something negative, we act in the opposite way. We convince ourselves and others that we genuinely feel the opposite of what we truly do, making this a deeper form of denial.

Reaction formation is often supported and even expected by society. For example, if our mom tells us that good little girls don't lose their temper, we might internalize that message. When we feel upset or angry, instead of showing our irritation, we act happy and content. We suppress our real feelings and hide the parts of ourselves that don't seem acceptable to others, putting up a façade that we believe is more appropriate.

SUBLIMATION

Finally, there is sublimation, another personal favorite. Sublimation occurs when we take an unwanted desire or feeling and channel it into a more socially acceptable outlet. For example, if we feel intensely angry, we can put all of that anger into action at work and get a promotion. When we're overwhelmed by stress, we might choose to go for a run instead of confronting our feelings head-on. In many ways, our society praises and even rewards this type of behavior. I used to exercise as a way to avoid admitting that I was hurt, angry, or upset. My friends would praise my dedication to health and fitness, but in reality I wasn't focused on fitness at all—I was using it to avoid dealing with the emotions I needed to face.

Sublimation can be deceptive because it often appears to be something positive, like health or resilience, when instead, it's just another way we hide our true selves or feelings. It allows us to be accepted and loved, which can sometimes feel more important or safer than being authentic.

PROTECTOR PARTS

Regardless of which defense mechanism we choose on any given day, the important thing to recognize here is that it serves a purpose. It makes us feel more acceptable, lovable, and in control of things. For me, the key was noticing when I was being defensive and realizing what was beneath it. Instead of letting my defenses run the show, push people away, or hide what was going on, I tried to figure out what I was running from. If I was intellectualizing, I had to think about why I was choosing to think instead of feel. Was it because I was experiencing an emotion I didn't like? Was it because that emotion wasn't "good" or might reflect poorly on who I should be? If I didn't know why I was doing it, there was no way I was going to be able to figure out how to stop it, right?

Each of these defense mechanisms exists to protect us, likely because we've been hurt in the past when we expressed ourselves openly and without hesitation. If we try to stop using them by simply judging ourselves for even having that urge, we're actually continuing the harm we've experienced. Instead of breaking the cycle, we reinforce the idea that our true feelings are unacceptable, further disconnecting from our authentic selves.

To help better manage our defense mechanisms, because they'll never go away completely, it's important to consider thanking them for all they've done. I know that sounds odd, but these mechanisms have protected us and helped us survive. It's important to acknowledge that. Think of them as an overzealous watchdog that alerts us to every little noise and movement. Our defense mechanisms are always on high alert and ready to protect us. Once we recognize them for what they are, our frontline defenders, we can thank them for showing up and gently tell them it's okay to stand down. By doing this, we can start to respond to situations more thoughtfully, rather than reacting out of habit.

LETTING YOUR GUARD DOWN

Not reacting and instead responding thoughtfully sounds great, calm even, but when I first started doing this, it was anything but. In the beginning, trying to pause and think before reacting felt incredibly awkward and uncomfortable. I would toggle between wanting to intellectualize my experience and knowing that I shouldn't. Then I'd get mad at myself for having such a tough time and I would take it all out on my husband. It was as if I was trying to swim against a strong current, with my instincts pushing me to react impulsively while I struggled to find a more measured approach.

I'd find myself stuck in the tension of wanting to maintain my old habits of immediate, defensive reactions, while also trying to practice this new way of responding. The process often felt like a battle within myself—my emotions would surge, and the old patterns of defensiveness and toxic independence would flare up. Every attempt to pause and think through my responses felt like I was stumbling through a maze, unsure of where the path would lead or whether I could navigate it successfully.

Thankfully, I had a breakthrough. One evening I was upset with my husband, Sean, and I started acting passive-aggressively. I quickly found myself back in the cycle I had been working so hard to break. I decided I was sick of it and I was just going to tell him how I felt. I wanted to explain why my feelings were hurt and apologize for the way I had been acting. Guess what? He responded lovingly, apologized for hurting my feelings, and we both felt better.

It sounds simple, maybe even obvious, but it was a huge moment for me. I didn't jump to protect myself, stuff down how I felt, and push through. I allowed myself to be exposed, honest, and authentic. Instead of pushing him away, I let him in, and it changed everything. By letting him in, I realized that vulnerability didn't weaken me, it strengthened our connection. It showed me that being honest about my feelings not only allowed me to be seen and understood but also gave Sean a chance to show up for me in a way I hadn't allowed before. That moment was a turning point in our relationship and my journey toward healthier emotional expression. It was proof that real intimacy is built on openness, not defensiveness.

BEING KNOWN

It's terrifying to be yourself sometimes. I think because we worry that if we truly show someone who we are, they might not accept us. That potential rejection can be scary and we can believe that we can't survive it. Yet if we don't allow ourselves to be known, we may never feel like we belong.

There's something profoundly life-affirming about feeling seen, heard, and understood. It's easy to overlook the importance of these feelings, assuming they are just basic needs. But taking a moment to reflect on what they really mean is crucial. To feel seen is not just about someone being able to describe what we look like; it's about being recognized for who we are, what we do, and the value we bring to the world. It means that someone truly understands us and accepts us completely, beyond surface-level interactions. When we experience this depth of connection, it validates our existence and reinforces our sense of worth, making us feel genuinely included and significant.

Feeling heard goes beyond simply having someone listen to us; it involves them actively engaging with our thoughts and feelings. When we feel heard, it means that someone is truly paying attention. They're not just waiting for their turn to speak, but fully absorbing and acknowledging what we're communicating. I worked on a video years ago about listening, and how we often listen to win or listen to fix, when the only way to successfully hear someone is when we listen to learn. When it feels like someone is focused, wanting to know more about us, and asking thoughtful follow-up questions, that's when we feel heard.

I believe that feeling seen and heard are prerequisites to feeling understood. Feeling understood is about more than just having someone grasp the surface of what we're going through. It means they have an empathetic knowledge of our inner world, our struggles, our dreams, and the complexities of our experiences. When we feel understood, it's as though someone has touched the very essence of who we are. They see past the façades we wear and recognize the depths of our vulnerabilities and aspirations. This profound connection affirms that our innermost feelings are not only valid but deeply acknowledged. It's a sanctuary where we can be our true selves without fear of judgment or rejection. Feeling understood is a rare and precious gift, a reminder that despite our individual journeys, we are never truly alone.

These vital feelings—being seen, heard, and understood—cannot exist without vulnerability. To truly connect with others, we must be willing to reveal the layers of our inner selves, to share our stories, fears, and dreams. Vulnerability is the bridge between our solitary experiences and the profound intimacy we seek in relationships. It can be a terrifying leap, as it means exposing our rawest selves and allowing the possibility of hurt and disappointment. Yet vulnerability is the only currency that deep, meaningful relationships accept. It's daring to show up as our true selves, despite the risk of being misunderstood or rejected.

By opening ourselves up to the chance of emotional pain, we make room for a richer connection, one that is grounded in authenticity and trust. This willingness to be vulnerable allows others to truly see us, to listen deeply, and to understand us in ways that superficial interactions never could. It is through this courageous act of sharing our innermost selves that we pave the way for deep, lasting bonds.

To grow and improve our lives we are going to have to let down our guard and show our true selves. It's scary and difficult, and I still find myself reaching for those old defense mechanisms that kept me safe but alone all those years. But if we keep doing the same thing, we will keep getting the same result. I know that some of you may think it's easier to just keep people away, that isolation feels safer, so why change? The reality is that no one said you had to, but I want you to be honest with yourself. Does isolation really feel good? Is this the life you dreamed of for yourself? Or is it possible that you haven't tried to connect with others because that would mean you would have to work on yourself?

So often we convince ourselves that we are better off without others because letting them in would force us to confront our faults. Don't let your fear of vulnerability keep you from experiencing meaningful connections. By pushing people away, we avoid the discomfort of self-examination, but we also miss out on the opportunity for growth and authentic relationships. Embracing the possibility of being seen, heard, and understood, despite our imperfections, opens the door to deeper, more rewarding connections that can enrich our lives in ways we never thought possible. Take the chance—you are worth knowing.

"WHY DO I KEEP DOING THIS?" EXERCISE—*QUESTIONS TO BETTER UNDERSTAND AND MANAGE OUR DEFENSES*

1. How does defensiveness serve as a protective mechanism and a barrier to meaningful connection in your life?

2. In what ways have you used emotional distance to create a sense of safety? How has this affected your relationships?
3. When has feeling "in control" through defensiveness offered you a sense of security, and when did you realize it was limiting your growth?
4. What are the potential risks of allowing yourself to be truly known by others? How do these risks compare to the benefits of vulnerability?
5. Can you recall moments when your defensiveness was justified? How can you distinguish between healthy self-protection and unhealthy isolation?
6. How do you imagine your relationships would change if you stopped relying on defensiveness as a form of self-protection?

CONTROL CHALLENGE

For the next **three days**, try this:

Notice the urge to control: When someone gives you feedback, asks a personal question, or disagrees with you, pause. Instead of reacting defensively, ask yourself: "Am I trying to control how they see me or how I feel?"

Reframe the discomfort: If you feel defensive, reframe it as **an opportunity to learn** rather than a threat. Ask: "What's the fear behind my reaction? What if I didn't have to protect myself right now?"

Practice intentional vulnerability: Choose **one small moment** to be open where you'd normally be defensive—whether it's admitting you don't know something, sharing a real feeling, or resisting the urge to explain yourself.

At the end of the three days, reflect:

- What changed when you let go of control over how others perceive you?
- Did defensiveness protect you, or did vulnerability create more connection?

Small shifts like these can help loosen the grip of defensiveness while allowing you to feel safer in your own skin.

Chapter 9

FITTING IN AND FEELING LEFT OUT

Why Belonging Is Vitally Important

I RECENTLY MOVED TO ANOTHER STATE, ONE THAT ISN'T USUALLY thrilled about Californians relocating here. Partly it's because we're moving in such large numbers, but there's also a feeling that we differ in social and political views. This tension made driving around with California plates risky. There were times we got honked at or cut off on the road. We moved quickly to change our plates and driver's licenses and, honestly, I felt a certain relief once we did. Somehow, blending in by "passing" as someone from that state, though I don't see myself as one, makes me feel safer, like I'm a little less exposed.

Yet an interesting shift happens when I leave and someone asks me where I'm from. I should say the current state I'm living in, because that's home now, but I hesitate. The words feel somehow untrue, like I can't bring myself to claim them. It's as if my quick urge to adapt here has left me feeling a bit lost, or at least inauthentic.

This isn't entirely new, though. Growing up, all I wanted was to blend in seamlessly to avoid standing out or drawing attention.

Anything that made me different felt risky, like it would expose me. So I controlled my quirks by hiding them, tucked away my unique interests, and did whatever I could to fit in, believing that camouflaging myself would protect me from judgment, rejection, or that uncomfortable feeling of being different. Now, even as an adult, I'm beginning to see how quickly this urge to belong can still come up, and how it sometimes leaves me wondering where, or even who, I really am.

My husband, Sean, often shares a story from when he was in preschool. They were teaching the kids how to snap their fingers, but he just couldn't get it right. Not wanting to stand out, he started making the sound of a snap with his mouth, hoping no one would notice he wasn't actually snapping. It was his way of blending in, of avoiding that feeling of being different or not good enough. And he's not alone. So many of us find little ways to hide our struggles or insecurities, whether pretending to know the answer in class or faking confidence in social situations.

I vividly remember begging my mom for Abercrombie jeans and Dr. Martens sandals because that's what everyone was wearing. When she told me they were too expensive, I saved up my allowance, determined to get them on my own, thinking that if I looked the part I would be accepted. So much of my teenage years were spent trying to fit in with the "cool" group, focusing on controlling and hiding anything about myself that didn't match what I thought was acceptable. I even remember getting a padded bra in middle school because all of the other girls had boobs and I was still flat-chested. Being unique or different seemed like the worst thing that could happen, so I pretended to be like everyone else to feel like I belonged.

My friend Jared shares a similar story:

> *When I was in fourth and fifth grade, around 1996, skateboarding was such a big thing for the cool boys in our school. There was a shop in my hometown that sold a ton of skateboarding items and I would always want to go there to buy clothes, but I didn't skateboard. One day I started buying and wearing the clothes in an attempt to fit in. I did this for about three or four months until one day at school someone said to me, "You don't even skateboard, why do you wear the clothes?" To which I quickly replied that "I do skateboard." When they asked me what board I used, I was so dumbfounded and didn't know how to answer. It was then that I was called a "poser" in front of several of my peers and I felt so embarrassed. From there, each artificial personality or identity I created is much more thoroughly thought through to protect my safety.*

I know things have changed since I was a kid, but fitting in is still a large part of how we navigate life. Whether it's through social media, workplace dynamics, or even friendships, we're constantly measuring ourselves against others, adjusting who we are to feel like we belong. It's easy to believe that as we grow older, we should naturally become more comfortable in our own skin. The truth is, the deep-seated need to be accepted doesn't just disappear. The fear of standing out, of being "othered," can still feel just as real as it did back in middle school.

IT'S BIOLOGICAL

This strong pull to fit in is deeply rooted in our biology. It's adaptive, wired into us for survival. For millions of years, being part of a group meant safety, protection, and a greater chance of existence. Acceptance by others wasn't just a matter of feeling good; it was essential. Being excluded or cast out could mean isolation, which was a real threat to survival in early human history. While we no longer face the same physical dangers, that evolutionary need to belong still drives much of our behavior today. It's why rejection or exclusion can feel so destabilizing; it taps into something primal within us.

At a fundamental level, we all share the human need not to feel alone in our struggles or in our way of being. We seek connection because it reassures us that we are not facing our challenges alone. It's comforting to know that others share our experiences, that our feelings are understood, and that our ways of navigating life are validated by those around us. This need for connection, rooted in our survival instincts, remains a powerful force throughout our lives. It's what drives much of our desire to fit in, because the pain of being left out or rejected can be profoundly scary, and at times feel threatening to our safety.

LOSING OURSELVES

When we do everything we can to control our natural instincts to fit in and look the part, we can start to lose touch with ourselves and who we are. At first, it may seem harmless, changing the way we dress, speak, or act to match those around us. But over time, these small adjustments can start to add up. We can begin to prioritize what others expect of us over what we truly want or believe, and that's when the disconnection begins.

The more we focus on fitting in, the further we distance ourselves from our authentic selves. We start to control and suppress parts of who we are, our unique opinions, interests, or quirks, if they don't align with the group's norms.

For example, my friend Holly shared that while her dad was a feminist (which had many positive aspects), as a little girl she loved pink, and princesses, and wanted to be a cheerleader. But those interests didn't fit with her dad's values, so she wasn't allowed to engage in them. As a child, she went along with it, but as an adult, she unconsciously built a personality that was logical and as far from femininity as possible. It wasn't until after her dad passed away that she realized she had repressed a whole part of herself. She still liked those "girly" things; she just hadn't allowed herself to embrace them.

This betrayal of our true self can lead to a kind of identity confusion. We become so accustomed to shaping ourselves based on others' expectations that we start to forget who we are. Over time, we can struggle to answer simple questions about what *we* enjoy, what *we* value, and what *we* stand for, because we've been so busy being someone else. Just like Terry from my community shared:

> *For most of my life, I tried so hard to fit in that I lost sight of who I actually was. I'd change the way I dressed, talked, or even the things I liked, depending on the people around me. I even ate foods I hated because it was what everyone else said they wanted!*
>
> *At some point, I became so good at adapting that I forgot what I truly enjoyed, and valued, and what made me unique. Now, in my late thirties, I find myself struggling to answer simple questions like "What do I like?" or "What makes me happy?" It's unsettling to realize that after all this time, I don't know who I am.*

As we lose touch with our true selves, we can also lose our inner compass, the sense of knowing what's right or meaningful for us. When we constantly look to others for validation or approval, we often stop listening to our intuition. This can make it hard to make decisions or stand up for ourselves because we no longer trust our own judgment. We can become more reactive to external influences, doing what's expected instead of what feels right for us. This can lead to feelings of confusion, self-doubt, or even resentment as we realize we've been living according to other people's rules rather than our own.

The emotional impact of this disconnection can be profound. When we suppress parts of ourselves, it creates an internal conflict. We're constantly trying to keep up appearances while ignoring our true needs and feelings. This can lead to anxiety, depression, or even a sense of emptiness, because even if we "fit in," we're not being accepted for who we are. We're essentially playing a role, and any sense of belonging we achieve can feel hollow because it's based on a false version of ourselves. This kind of inauthentic connection can actually make us feel more isolated and alone because deep down we know that we're not being seen or understood.

Trying to fit in at all costs may give us temporary relief, the feeling of being accepted, even if it's superficial. But the long-term consequences can be devastating. In friendships, relationships, and even at work, we might find that people are drawn to the version of us that we've crafted to please them, not the real us. This can lead to shallow or unfulfilling connections because there's no genuine foundation of understanding or mutual acceptance. We can end up feeling trapped in a persona we created, unable to break free because we fear that showing our true selves will lead to rejection. The irony is that, in our attempt to avoid rejection, we've rejected ourselves in the process.

THE NEED TO BE LIKED

I've struggled most with the urge to "fit in" in my romantic relationships. It may seem surprising, but the intimacy and vulnerability involved made them feel riskier, as if rejection in that context would hurt even more. I'd pretend to enjoy a sport I didn't care for, dress in ways that didn't reflect my true style, and even hold back my opinions just to keep someone around. Over time, I realized that I didn't even like the people I was dating. We had nothing in common, and they really didn't know anything about me. I had molded myself so much to fit into their world that I lost sight of my own. It became clear that I wasn't just faking interest in a few things here and there; I was building entire relationships based on a version of me that didn't exist. When those relationships inevitably ended, one of my go-to mantras was, "They didn't even know me," and honestly, that couldn't have been more true. I had controlled and kept my real self so hidden that I wasn't giving them, or myself, a chance to truly connect.

I'm still not entirely sure why I did this for so long. Maybe it was because I wanted to believe I was lovable, that people liked me, and that I could fit into their world. I craved that validation so much that I was willing to compromise who I was, hoping that if I could just be the version they wanted, I'd finally feel accepted. But in the process, I lost sight of the fact that being truly loved means being seen for who you are, not for who you think others want you to be. I had multiple long-term relationships, all of which ended, and in none of which I felt seen and understood. I felt more alone than ever.

I remember realizing this pattern in one of my last long-term relationships before meeting my husband. In an effort to correct my errors, I started trying to be myself. I began standing up for myself more and sharing my opinions and thoughts. I hoped that the relationship would deepen, and all of the faking would just be forgotten. Instead, I felt a chasm form almost immediately. He didn't understand why I was acting the way I was and assumed I was doing it to punish him or be obstinate. Needless to say, our relationship devolved and we broke up. He didn't know who I was, and it was clear that I couldn't be who I was with him. In all honesty, if I had been myself from the beginning, we would've never dated in the first place.

It took me a while to get over that breakup, not because I thought he was the one or was in love with him, but because it seemed to support my belief that being myself wasn't a good thing. I believed that without altering who I was, I would be cast out or rejected, and that was gut-wrenching. I debated whether I should go back to controlling, pretending, thinking it might protect me from rejection and give me the validation I desperately needed. But I couldn't do it. I knew how uncomfortable it was, and I realized that if my mask slipped, it could end any relationship I had begun. That fear felt just as terrifying.

As much as I wanted to blame all of these failed relationships on the guys I was with, in the end, I realized it had nothing to do with them and everything to do with my view of self. If I kept believing that I wasn't good enough as I was, I would never feel safe to be myself. This realization marked the beginning of a new chapter for me, where instead of hiding away in another fake relationship, I tried to turn my focus to the things I enjoyed. I also made more time for my friendships and took a step back from dating altogether.

This break from romantic relationships provided the space I needed to explore who I was and try to learn to appreciate and love myself. Sure, I found out that I can be stubborn and annoying at times, but I also discovered qualities about myself that I genuinely like and value. Embracing all the parts of myself that I thought weren't okay or acceptable has been tough, and I am still navigating it, but I can say that finding someone who loves you for your true-at-home-alone self, well, there's nothing like it.

SHOULDING ALL OVER

Recently, I was watching a rerun of *Sex and the City* where the character Miranda is on her honeymoon with her husband, Steve. They go to a mountain retreat in Upstate New York, where there's no TV, no internet, and nothing to do but spend time together. She calls her friends to complain about how bored she is, joking that she can't just have sex all weekend and that three days of this quiet retreat are too much for her. Almost as soon as she says it, though, she backtracks, insisting she *should* be enjoying herself; it's her honeymoon, after all, and it's supposed to be romantic.

Miranda's use of the word "should" is a perfect example of another way we disconnect from our true selves. The moment she says "should," she's no longer expressing her actual feelings but rather what she believes she *ought* to feel based on society's expectations. She's shifting into a control pattern. It's as if there's no room to deviate from the script. We're conditioned to think that if something is considered ideal or romantic, we're obligated to feel that way too, even if our idea of romance is completely different. When we *should* all over ourselves and our lives, we lose touch with our authentic emotions and experiences and force ourselves to fall in line with what we think is expected of us.

Three years ago, Sean and I moved to a new state and bought our first home. We were thrilled and proud to take this next step. However, I didn't fully anticipate how jarring this transition would be for me. Even though I feel like I *should* be happy about our new home and life in the suburbs, compared to the bustling city of Santa Monica, California, I am not. The two cities couldn't be more different, and I feel incredibly out of place. This sense of disconnection is the strongest I've felt since my teenage years.

When I tried to share these feelings with people in my life, I was often met with comments about how beautiful our new house is and how much there is to be grateful for. And while I appreciate these positive reflections, they didn't address the deep sense of displacement I was experiencing. It's been a struggle to reconcile the gap between what I *should* feel and what I actually feel. And I find myself unsure of how to move forward. If I fight to fit in, I will leave my true self out in the cold, but if I don't, I will continue feeling isolated and alone. It feels like I am hurting myself either way, and if you've ever experienced this, you know just how heavy and hopeless this can feel.

THE IMPORTANCE OF CONNECTION

Whether we want to admit it or not, we all crave connection. Our nervous system is wired to be soothed through it. Dr. Stephen Porges's polyvagal theory highlights how our autonomic nervous system is intricately designed to respond to social interactions. According to this theory,[1] our bodies are equipped with a sophisticated system for detecting safety and connection through the vagus nerve. When we engage in meaningful, vulnerable interactions, our parasympathetic nervous system is activated, promoting a state of calm and safety. This physiological response not only helps regulate our stress levels but also fosters deeper emotional bonds. In essence, our craving for genuine connection is not just a psychological desire but a fundamental biological need, as our nervous system thrives on the reassurance and intimacy that comes from being truly seen and understood.

Feeling isolated or "othered" is upsetting for many reasons. One that is often overlooked is the impact on our nervous system. Our sense of safety and connection is intricately linked to the state of our autonomic nervous system. When we feel isolated or disconnected, it activates our body's stress response, shifting us into a state of heightened alertness or even freeze.

Conversely, when we experience genuine connection and acceptance, our vagal tone is positively engaged, which activates the parasympathetic nervous system. This response promotes a state of calm, safety, and openness, allowing us to feel secure enough to engage with others. It fosters a sense of trust and well-being, making social interaction more enjoyable and effortless. Over time, these positive experiences strengthen our vagal tone, enhancing our ability to regulate emotions, respond to stress, and maintain meaningful relationships.

Understanding this physiological response helps explain why feeling out of place or rejected isn't just an emotional challenge but a biological one. It underscores the importance of fostering environments where we feel safe and accepted, not only for our emotional well-being but also for our physiological health.

THE PARADOX

The tricky thing about polyvagal theory is that it underscores the vital importance of genuine connection for our overall well-being. However, if we don't feel connected, our nervous system's stress response can drive us to seek connection in ways that may not fulfill our need for real and meaningful interactions. This can lead to a paradox where, in our desperation to feel connected, we might engage in controlling behaviors that prevent us from forming the authentic relationships we need. The very urgency we feel to connect can hinder our ability to get it. It's like we get stuck in a cycle of disconnection or fake connection, and it's hard to get out of it.

> *I have been trying to meet more people and make more friends, so I am constantly signing up for every social event and joining all these online groups. My therapist keeps telling me that I need more social support, so I am really trying. I figured if I just kept busy and put myself out there, I'd eventually find my people and fit in. But it hasn't worked yet, and I am honestly losing hope. I swear I feel more alone now than I did before I started working on it. It's so frustrating.*

> *I even recently went to this party, full of people I kinda knew but am not close to (most of them I know from work). I spent the whole night making small talk, trying to laugh at the right moments and blend in. But by the end of it, I felt more alone than when I first got there. It was like I was chasing new friendships so hard, but all I got were these surface-level interactions that left me feeling empty.*

That's exactly what I have been struggling with. Fighting so hard to find my place here, and instead of feeling seen and understood, I just feel more alone. In an effort to save myself, I say yes to any invitation, even if I'm not genuinely interested in what they're doing. I thought that by keeping busy and saying yes, I'd eventually find my people and feel connected. But what has happened is that I end up in situations where I'm not myself, trying to fit into places where I don't belong. It's exhausting and futile, and it leaves me feeling even more isolated because I'm not connecting in a way that's authentic to who I am. It's like I'm doing all the right things to try and belong, but I'm still missing out on that real, deep connection I'm craving.

FINDING YOUR PEOPLE

While I would love to tell you that I have a quick fix for all our connection problems, unfortunately, I don't. The only solution I've found so far is to travel back to Santa Monica more often to visit my close friends regularly. I have realized that I need the reminder that I am seen and understood by people, even if they don't live next door to me anymore. It's like the comfort of a familiar dish from a favorite restaurant; even if I can't have it every day, having it occasionally reminds me of what I'm missing and helps me appreciate it more. This experience has shown me that while we might not always be able to fully re-create the past, we can still seek out and nurture relationships that make us feel valued and understood. It's about finding ways to stay connected to what genuinely fulfills us, even when our circumstances change. Yes, it's difficult, but in my experience, it's vital.

However, I understand that some of us might not have close, familiar people to turn to, or may have never felt truly connected and aren't sure where to begin. Don't worry, I do have some strategies that can help you build connections, along with some common pitfalls to avoid based on my missteps.

First, consider engaging in activities or joining groups related to your interests or passions. Whether it's a hobby, a class, or a community event, these are great places to meet people with similar interests. This is why, when I started saying yes to things I didn't even enjoy, I struggled to find my people; we didn't have anything in common! Authentic connections often begin with shared experiences, and they naturally lead to meaningful conversations. I find that this can help us get to know people without any pressure. If we come across an attribute that we don't like or that doesn't align with us, we can easily end that relationship when the class or event ends.

While it can still be difficult to leave the house and put ourselves out there, especially after the last few years post-COVID, I cannot encourage you enough to get out, try new things, and see what happens. We don't have to stay in a class if we hate it or continue to play guitar if we don't enjoy it, but we are going to have to do something different if we want things to change. Like Brené Brown says, "We can choose courage, or we can choose comfort, but we can't have both. Not at the same time."[2] If we want more connection than we have, we are going to have to find new ways of getting it.

Second, don't underestimate the power of small, everyday interactions. These seemingly minor moments, like sharing a smile with someone as you walk toward the same sandwich shop or engaging in a brief conversation with a neighbor while grabbing your mail, can be more significant than they appear. These casual exchanges can open doors to genuine connections and friendships. Being open to starting conversations with neighbors, colleagues, or even people you encounter in everyday settings can lead to surprising and meaningful connections.

That's actually how I met my one and only friend where I live now. She's my neighbor, and when we were both out walking our dogs, I struck up a conversation with her about our pets and the neighborhood. That small, friendly chat eventually turned into regular hangouts while our dogs played together, and now we've built a real friendship. It reminded me how just being open and approachable can create unexpected connections. You might find common ground with someone you see regularly at your local coffee shop, and a friendly chat could evolve into a regular meetup or a new friendship. Similarly, a simple greeting or question to a coworker you've only briefly interacted with could lead to a deeper understanding and connection over time.

Sometimes, the most meaningful relationships begin with these small, everyday interactions. They can be the foundation for building a supportive community and discovering shared interests or experiences. They are also simple and don't take much time or energy. By being open and approachable in these moments, you invite opportunities for connection that might otherwise be missed, enriching your social life in unexpected ways.

Third, be proactive in reaching out and making plans. I'll admit, I'm not great at this, but I've been working on it because I'm always glad when I do. I make it a point to text friends, check their availability, and set up plans. Knowing that these plans are scheduled for the future often makes them feel less overwhelming at the moment, and it gives me something to look forward to. Even if I feel hesitant or tempted to cancel on the day of the event, I remind myself that pushing through always boosts my mood.

So don't hesitate to take the initiative, whether inviting someone for coffee, texting that friend you haven't seen in a while, or attending a social gathering. Taking these steps shows that you're interested in building connections and can lead to meaningful relationships. The effort you put into reaching out and making plans can open doors to new opportunities and enrich your social life. Remember, it's often the small, proactive actions that help strengthen our connections and make our social interactions more fulfilling.

Finally, be patient with yourself and others. Building genuine connections is a process that unfolds over time. It's important to remember that it's perfectly okay if things don't click immediately. Everyone has their own pace and rhythm, and relationships often require time to develop naturally. Give yourself grace as you navigate these interactions, and don't be discouraged if a connection doesn't form right away or if you realize it's not working. Keep putting yourself out there, and trust that your efforts are building a foundation for meaningful relationships. It's through these gradual and authentic exchanges that you'll find people who truly appreciate you for who you are.

Every step you take toward reaching out and being open is valuable. Even if it feels like progress is slow, each interaction helps you learn more about yourself and others and brings you closer to finding those who resonate with your true self. Be kind to yourself on this journey and know that your patience and persistence will eventually lead to deeper, more fulfilling connections. And, if it helps, know that I am right there with you.

RECLAIMING OUR AUTHENTICITY

In high school, I did something unusual. A fellow student, who I had a few classes with, told me that many of my friends had been bullying her and calling her names. At first, I was skeptical, but as I started paying closer attention to how my friends treated others, I realized that her claims were true. Their behavior was appalling, and I found myself feeling embarrassed to be associated with them. Instead of confronting them or discussing the issue, I stopped reaching out and making plans with them. I now recognize that I should have talked with them and let them know that their behavior wasn't okay. At the time I was only fifteen and this felt like the easiest option. I gradually distanced myself from the group without any confrontation. I had almost forgotten about this until recently when my mom reminded me of it. She pointed out that I had told her I didn't want to see those friends anymore, and that's exactly what I did.

This experience marked a significant moment in my life. I was beginning to understand that friendships that don't align with my values and who I want to be aren't worth having. More importantly, I was willing to put faith in myself and know that I would be okay without them. That's the hardest part, because that connection is so vital, and it can feel scary to move away from what we know. But even as a teen I knew who I was, and sadly, that didn't line up with that friend group.

Looking back, I am both shocked and proud of teenage Kati for making such a bold choice. It's remarkable to see how even then, I dared to prioritize my values over social acceptance. That decision, though seemingly simple, was difficult and took a lot of confidence to make. I remember thinking I would be okay because I was friendly to everyone (hello, people-pleaser), but it was still a rough transition. In a way, I think my empathy was what gave me the push to do it, because I couldn't get over how pained that girl looked when she told me about the things they said and did to her. I had to get as far away from them as possible.

In the end, that experience taught me an invaluable lesson about the importance of self-respect and integrity. It wasn't easy to let go of those friendships or my need for their approval, but it was a crucial step in learning to value my own beliefs and feelings over external validation. It reinforced the idea that true connection and acceptance come from relinquishing control and being genuine, not from conforming to others' expectations. This early experience of standing up for my values has shaped how I approach friendships and self-acceptance today, reminding me that embracing who I am, even when it's uncomfortable, is always worth the effort.

WHERE WE BELONG

Needing community and connection is always going to be something we crave; it's hardwired into our nervous system. We can't deny it. However, we can't settle for relationships that aren't founded on our authentic selves. We know that those types of connections don't give us the same safe and secure feeling as those built on honesty and mutual respect. When we present ourselves as someone we're not, we're constantly managing an exhausting façade, and over time, that leaves us feeling more isolated and disconnected than before.

But figuring out where we belong isn't always easy. It's tempting to mold ourselves to fit into places we think we should be or to stay in relationships that feel comfortable even if they aren't aligned with who we truly are. What we often fail to realize is that real connection, the kind that fulfills and sustains us, can only be found when we allow ourselves to show up authentically.

This is why finding where we truly belong starts with figuring out who we are. It might seem like we should just know ourselves, but so often, we get caught up in our to-do lists, responsibilities, and the expectations of others. In the process, we lose touch with what matters to us, our values, interests, and passions. To find belonging, we first need to reconnect with ourselves, understand what we need, and embrace our true identity rather than shape ourselves to fit in with others.

There are many ways we can do this, but there are two ways I have personally found to be the most effective.

The first is to take yourself out on some dates. We talked about this a little already, but we often think dates have to be romantic and include someone else. What if you took yourself out to do something you thought you might like? What would you do? Where would you go? How long would you stay? All of the details associated with a date, which are usually connected to getting to know a potential partner, can be applied to ourselves.

We can have bad dates where we don't like the location or the food is bad, and we can end those early. Or we can have great dates where we end up remembering something about ourselves and how we enjoy spending our time. All of these dates with ourselves can help us learn more about who we are and what we enjoy. I know it sounds silly, but figuring out who we are can seem like an impossible task, and this can make it feel more doable, maybe even fun.

The second tip that has helped me learn more about myself is taking stock of my values. Sounds simple enough, but it has been one of the most difficult and rewarding things I have done recently. "Values" is a word we use easily, but when trying to decide what my top five were, I was quickly overwhelmed. I mean, I know I value consistency and loyalty, but are those really in my top five? It was hard to even know where to start, so I just began writing down as many values as I could think of and crossing off the ones that didn't feel good to me. That helped me narrow it down to about twenty, and then I realized that many of the values I was drawn to had similar roots.

The few values that truly resonated with me, things I personally strived for and sought in others, centered around three key principles:

community, consistency, and comfort. I had three of my top five already squared away. Then I ran into another issue: What things do I value because someone else told me I should? There's that *should* word again, telling me that I could have accepted certain values because I thought that they were what was most acceptable.

This brings me to where I am in my process now, trying to untangle the values I truly hold with those that have been imposed upon me. Things like "productivity" and "financial success" may not be things I value, but are things I believe to be important within society. This part is tricky because I have spent a lot of my time and energy supporting these values, and I am not sure how to just switch that off. So far all I have figured out is that I can consciously decide to put more energy into the things that bring me closer to community, consistency, and comfort. In doing so I am hoping to get closer to who I really am.

To relieve some of the pressure you may feel to figure out precisely who you are and carve it in stone, know that it can change. Any of the values you come up with today may not hold up in a year or two. We may decide that comfort wasn't exactly what we wanted; instead, it was balance we were looking for. We aren't rigid or immovable, we are malleable and change shape over time. This is why I believe this step should be repeated regularly, especially when we feel lost or disconnected. It can serve as a beacon, guiding us back to ourselves.

Ultimately, we are trying to build a home within ourselves. When we know who we are and what we value, we can more easily navigate new connections. We can feel more empowered to start or end certain relationships trusting in our intuition. Yes, this takes time and practice, but building up our knowledge of self will help us navigate these situations with clarity and ease. Instead of being shaken by the fear of losing a relationship or ourselves, we can relax knowing that we have the tools to get back in touch with who we are. Doing so will give us the resilience to face life's uncertainties and create meaningful connections without losing ourselves in the process.

"WHY DO I KEEP DOING THIS?" EXERCISE— *QUESTIONS TO GET US THINKING ABOUT CONNECTION AND HOW IT'S AFFECTING US*

1. What does true connection feel like, and how do you know when you've found it?
2. In what situations do you feel most disconnected from others, and why do you think that happens?
3. When was a time you felt you truly belonged? What factors made that experience different?
4. What's the difference between being liked and feeling like you belong?
5. What are the moments in your life when you've felt most like yourself? What were the common threads?
6. What were the first few values that came to mind when reading this chapter? Why do you think those particular values stood out to you?

CONTROL CHALLENGE

Over the next week, choose one situation where you typically hold back or try to control your interactions (e.g., with a friend, family member, or coworker). In that moment, try something different:

Let go of control by allowing yourself to be vulnerable in that situation—whether it's sharing a personal thought, an emotion, or something that feels real for you.

Observe your feelings and responses: Notice how it feels to let go of control and how the other person responds. Is there a sense of relief, discomfort, or growth?

Journal your experience: Write down what happened, what you learned, and how it impacted your connection with that person. Did you feel more connected, or did it create more distance? Did you feel more like yourself?

This task will help you explore how letting go of the need to control interactions can either deepen connections or reveal areas where you may need to work on trust and vulnerability. The goal is to practice releasing control in a safe, manageable way and see how it feels to let connection happen naturally.

Chapter 10

DEPRESSION AND FEELING STUCK

When We Struggle to Find a Reason to Try

CHANGE IS HARD. WE ALL KNOW THAT ON SOME LEVEL, YET when we set out to improve ourselves and our lives, we somehow expect it to be linear, smooth, and logical. The truth is that's rarely the case. We fight against ingrained habits, emotional triggers, and deep-seated beliefs that pull us back to the familiar, even when we know it's unhealthy. Just because we want to change doesn't mean it comes easily. Sometimes it feels like the harder we try, the more stuck we become. It's like a finger trap: The more we attempt to pull free, the tighter it grips.

This struggle happens because so much of our behavior is deeply ingrained, shaped by years of experience, conditioning, and sometimes even trauma. Our habits and thought patterns become automatic, embedded in our subconscious, making them feel almost like second nature. We develop these patterns to cope, survive, or make sense of the world around us, even when they no longer serve us well. They may be unhealthy, but they're also familiar, and there's a certain comfort in that. Our brains are wired to favor what's known because it's predictable and less risky, even if it's causing us harm.

When we try to change, we aren't just battling surface-level habits—we're taking on years, sometimes decades, of neural pathways that have become deeply set in place. These pathways are reinforced every time we respond to a situation in the same way, whether that's shutting down emotionally, turning to unhealthy coping mechanisms, or repeating self-critical thoughts. Our brain defaults to these well-worn tracks because they've been traveled many times. The more ingrained they are, the harder it can feel to carve out new pathways or act in healthier ways.

That's where depression can complicate things. Depression, which you might experience as deep sadness, lethargy, or a lack of motivation, adds another layer to this struggle. It's important to note that depression is nuanced, and for the sake of this chapter, we'll use depression to refer to these feelings of sadness and apathy. This weight can feel paralyzing, making the effort to change even more daunting. It's as though the emotional inertia created by depression pulls us further into a state of stagnation, making it harder to take the steps necessary for growth.

TRYING TO MOVE

Feeling stuck can show up in so many ways: physically, emotionally, situationally, and more. Maybe we're literally stuck in a place we don't want to be or feel trapped in an environment that doesn't feel right. Sometimes it's a town or a community where we just can't find our footing or make connections, leaving us feeling out of place. It's like our current reality is something we can't escape, no matter how much we'd like to, and it's beyond our control.

Emotionally, feeling stuck can mean being in relationships that no longer support or fulfill us. We might feel obligated to stay, whether it's due to closeness, time, or even family ties, and we struggle to break free. Or maybe we feel like we've hit a wall in our lives where we've stopped growing. It's easy to feel held back by limiting beliefs or by others' expectations, keeping us small, stagnant, and afraid to challenge ourselves in new ways.

For me, the biggest example of feeling stuck has been connected to my recent move. I've mentioned this a few times throughout the book, but the feeling of being rooted somewhere I don't want to be has been a constant presence, showing up in different ways as I navigate this new chapter. Every day I'm reminded that I'm in a place that doesn't quite feel like home, and I've had to find ways to stay motivated and push through the discomfort of feeling so out of place.

As I sit with these feelings of being stuck, frustrated, impatient, and overwhelmed, it's easy to see why change feels so intimidating. Change means opening ourselves up to discomfort and uncertainty, and that often feels worse than staying put. The weight of despair and doubt can seem like a tether, keeping us from moving forward. We convince ourselves that staying here, in this known place—even if it's painful—feels safer than risking failure, disappointment, or loss.

STUCK IN THE MUD

Our internal battle can feel relentless—leaving us pulled in every direction. It can make us question our worth, feel anxious about the future, and worry about our relationships. We try to keep control of everything around us while feeling lost within ourselves, and it can keep us stuck in this push/pull between our current experience and where we want to be. To truly move forward, we have to find a way to release what no longer serves us. Letting go can be scary and can feel messy at first, yet it's the only way to create space for something better.

One member of my community shared a perfect analogy that captures this struggle. She compared it to walking through the mud while wearing rain boots, or wellies:

> *Being or feeling stuck is like walking through the mud while wearing wellies. The wellies (our life factors or behaviors) get stuck, and suddenly we're unable to move forward. To break free, we have to ditch the wellies and leave them behind. This can be difficult because our wellies were protecting us from getting muddy. Letting go can feel uncomfortable, but if we want to move forward, we have to face that mud in order to be set free.*

Her analogy hits home. Our "wellies" represent the familiar habits, beliefs, and behaviors that once felt protective, even if they're no longer helping us. They might shield us from discomfort, but they also keep us stuck. Moving forward is going to require us to leave those old, unhelpful behaviors and people behind. No matter how uncomfortable it feels, we can face the uncertainty that comes with change. We have to believe that it will all work out and that life's got our back, even if that's not easy.

IN THE FIGHT OF OUR LIVES

In many cases we're not just trying to change an isolated behavior, we're essentially rewiring our brains. This requires breaking the cycle of automatic responses and creating new patterns, which can feel uncomfortable and unnatural at first. We can feel like we don't know what to say; we worry we sound crazy, or that those we love won't tolerate this new way of acting. It's no wonder we often find ourselves stuck or retreating to old habits, even when we're consciously trying to do better. It can feel like we sort of hit a wall in our work, unable to move forward. We can be scared of taking the next step or afraid to leave a past version of ourselves behind. We can even start to question whether or not this change is necessary or if we are capable of doing it at all. It can feel like we are in an internal battle against ourselves, unsure of who we are rooting for.

Change can feel like a fight because, in many ways, it is. It's a fight against the parts of ourselves that have grown attached to the familiar, the safe, and the predictable. It's a fight against long-held beliefs about who we are and what we deserve. And most of all, it's a fight against the deeply embedded wiring in our brains that resists the unfamiliar territory of transformation. All of this battling can be exhausting and leave us feeling stagnant, unsure of whether it's worth it. We can wonder if we are worth it.

As we wrestle with these old patterns, the sheer effort it takes can drain us emotionally and physically. Every day can feel like an uphill climb, trying to be more mindful, trying to break habits, trying to think differently, and it's relentless. The energy we put into fighting our natural tendencies can leave us feeling depleted. We might begin to wonder why we're doing it in the first place, especially when the rewards of change don't come as quickly as we'd hoped (life can be annoying that way). The desire for growth can start to feel more like a burden than an inspiration. We can feel stuck and hopeless. Just like this member of my community shared:

> *I feel like I just want to give up. I am trying all of the things my therapist said to do. I am journaling, doing my breathing exercises, making sure to get enough sleep, trying to reach out to friends I have lost touch with, you name it, I am trying it. But I still feel like shit. I have been working to get better for months*

and I just don't feel any different. Part of me thinks it would've been better if I never decided to start therapy. Like ignorance is bliss, because I did feel better back then, or at least I wasn't so aware of how bad I felt. Ugh. I don't know, it's just exhausting.

THIS SUCKS

Even as I write this, I realize how sad this can be. It is frustrating and steals our motivation to keep trying. The idea that change is such a slow, painful process can feel heavy, like it's sucking the air out of the room. It's disheartening to know that even with the best intentions and all the effort in the world, real transformation takes time, often more time than we're prepared for. And yet I know deep down that this struggle is part of the process. Change is rarely a quick fix or a smooth path, and I logically accept that. But still, there's a part of me that wishes it wasn't this way. I wish growth could be faster and more straightforward, without all the setbacks and detours that make it feel like two steps forward, one step back.

It's in those moments of slow progress that we can lose hope. I'm working hard to stop being such a people-pleaser, but the process has been slow and at times painfully difficult. I try to set boundaries, to say no when I need to, and to focus on my own needs rather than constantly putting others first. But it's exhausting, and sometimes I wonder if I'll ever get there. If it were just a matter of flipping a switch, it would be easier to manage. But unlearning these patterns is complicated, and progress feels like it's moving at a snail's pace. Sometimes I want to throw in the towel, let the negativity take over, and stop trying. But deep down, I know that mindset won't get me where I want to go. I have to hold on, keep looking for the good things, and put one foot in front of the other. Just like this member of my community shares:

> *I have felt stuck in therapy because *I* want to do the work, but my body isn't ready. Like two people holding hands: One person wants to go one direction, and the other pulls a different way. I've learned to be patient with "all of me" and understand that progress will only be made when I am wholly ready to take another step. As much as it is slower than I anticipated, it is still forward momentum, and I hold on to that.*

The slow pace of change and growth can be difficult to accept, and even more daunting to push through. How do we stay motivated when it feels like nothing is improving? Or worse, when it feels like things are getting even harder? It's in those moments when doubt creeps in, whispering that it would be easier to stop fighting for what we want. The temptation to settle for where we are, even if it's not what we truly desire, becomes so strong.

WHAT ARE YOU SO AFRAID OF?

It's during times of questioning our path forward that the real issues rear their ugly heads. Our deepest fears rise to the surface, and they can paralyze us, bringing our slow progress to a complete halt. These fears often revolve around how the people we love will react to the changes we're making. Will they still accept us?

When we fight to change the way we think and behave, it often means our relationships will shift, and sometimes they will end. This can be terrifying. We worry about being left alone, isolated, and misunderstood. Just like that story I told you about how my old boyfriend couldn't understand why I was acting differently. He pushed back against the changes I was making, and ultimately we broke up. Fearing the loss that may come with growth is natural, especially if we've experienced it before. Just like this member of my community shares about her fear of change ruining her relationship:

> *I feel like the epitome of "stuck." I'm in my forties and just now am dealing with the emotionally unavailable parents I had during childhood. I also chose a spouse who is the same. This led to decades of unprocessed traumas and emotions. My coping skills have been unhealthy and include disordered eating, self-hatred, and self-harm. I am working so hard to process these emotions, but when I make progress, I seem to stall and get stuck in the muck because my environment and situation will not change in the foreseeable future. In my mind, making any big changes will too greatly affect my family members and is nonnegotiable. This triggers hopelessness, which in turn amps up the unhealthy coping skills and then continues to cycle. I hope I can learn how to see and cope in my situation differently and discover how to break free!*

I came across a post online that said, "We had the most friends when we were the worst version of ourselves." While I don't fully agree, there is some truth in that. When we lack healthy boundaries or always put others first, we can attract people who are happy to take advantage of that. When we're younger and still figuring out who we are, we tend to appeal to a larger group because we're less discerning about who we let into our lives. Growth often means refining our relationships and becoming more selective about who gets access to us. It can feel lonely at first, but it's also part of becoming more authentic and surrounding ourselves with people who truly support the version of us we're striving to be.

As we figure out what's important, start valuing ourselves, and making positive change, not everyone is going to stay along for the ride. I am here to tell you that even though it's scary, it is okay. If we are honest with ourselves, we'll likely realize that relationships that don't align with who we are or support our growth aren't worth having. If we have people in our lives who depend on us staying the same forever, how is that sustainable? Putting some distance between ourselves and these relationships, if we're not able to fully limit our interactions, will help us to create space for those who do fully support our growth.

THE WANT

Starting the process of change or healing can feel overwhelming, especially when we're not entirely sure what the end goal looks like. Many of us think that to improve our lives or seek help, we need to be fully committed and have a clear vision of the future we want. But that's not always the case. Sometimes, the first step toward growth is simply acknowledging that our current situation is no longer sustainable. We may not know exactly what we want yet, but we do know that something has to change. It's this recognition—that we can't keep living the way we are—that can be the real catalyst for transformation.

I recently answered a question on a livestream from someone in my community who asked if she had to want to get better when starting therapy. The truth is, no, she doesn't have to be fully committed to change or have a clear desire to improve right from the start. What's more important is recognizing that the way things are now is no longer tolerable. In other words, to grow and improve, we don't necessarily need to have a strong, definitive desire for a better future. We just have to know that we can't keep living the way we are, and that can be the first step toward change.

As counterintuitive as it might sound, this is where I believe our depressive thoughts can serve a purpose. They can multitask beyond just being there to keep us stuck. These thoughts can highlight our discomfort and unhappiness, reminding us constantly of their presence. While depression often feels like a weight that holds us down and can be unbearable, the slightest lift in our symptoms can push us to take action. In that sense, the very thoughts that cause us pain can become motivators for change.

I know not everyone experiences depression in the same way, but the therapist in me can't help but reframe those negative symptoms. Instead of seeing them as obstacles, I view them as signals. They can be indicators of where our deepest struggles lie and, perhaps, sources of motivation to move toward something better. That discomfort, as painful as it is, can serve as a constant reminder of how bad things are. This in turn can push us to try harder, seek help, or make small changes. Sometimes it's not the hope for something better that drives us but the sheer determination to escape the way things are now.

THE UNKNOWN

Our fear of an unknown future can be a major obstacle to moving forward. It's easy to assume that when we're unhappy with our current life, the idea of change is exciting. In reality, the work that's often needed to move toward a "better" version of our life is unfamiliar, and that can be intimidating. Our brain and body are wired for safety, and part of staying safe means sticking to what we know.

Familiar situations help us prepare for interactions and plan what we want to say or do. When we've been through something before, it's not as frightening because we know how it plays out and how to respond. Even when those familiar situations are harmful or abusive, our brain and body often prefer them over something completely unknown. The fear of the unfamiliar can be stronger than the discomfort of staying where we are, even if where we are is hurting us. The unknown can feel scarier than the pain we're used to. That's why change, no matter how positive it might seem, can be hard to embrace.

When we're trying to chart a new path and fight for healthier changes in our lives, we can stall, freeze in fear, and start questioning whether we should even be doing this. The uncertainty of a new future, where things are different and unpredictable, can make us doubt our decisions. We might ask ourselves, "What if I fail? What if I lose people? What if things don't get better?" These questions fuel our hesitation, making us cling to the familiar, even when we know it's not serving us.

It's important to acknowledge that this fear is natural. Change pushes us out of our comfort zone, and with that comes a sense of vulnerability. We might feel exposed, and unsure of how to navigate new situations or relationships. The urge to go back to what we know can be overwhelming. At least in those familiar patterns we know what to expect. If we want to grow and truly heal, we have to push past that fear. Stepping into the unknown and embracing the discomfort of growth will give ourselves the chance to create a life that's not just familiar but fulfilling.

This part of the process feels like standing at the edge of a cliff, knowing I need to jump into the unknown, yet clinging to the safety of the familiar. It creates a cycle of doubt and frustration. I start questioning whether I'm even capable of trusting the process or if I'm just setting myself up for disappointment. The gap between knowing and doing has never been wider, but despite that, I know I can't stay where I am. It's like in those movie scenes when the ground beneath someone's feet is starting to crumble, but they're still too scared to jump.

But here's the reality: We don't have a choice. Staying where we are isn't an option anymore, and trying to control everything is only delaying the inevitable. At some point, we just have to take the leap, face the discomfort, and trust that it will all work out. Because in the end, the fear of jumping is far smaller than the pain of staying stuck. Yes, it's scary. But staying stuck in a cycle of pain or dissatisfaction is scarier in the long run. The key is to trust that the discomfort of change is temporary, while the benefits of growth and healthier choices will be long-lasting.

WHO AM I?

One hidden but crucial part of change is the fear of losing ourselves. When we're in that middle phase—aware we don't like where we are but not yet where we want to be—we can feel uncertain about who we even are. As we learn healthier ways to communicate with loved ones and improve our relationship with ourselves, nothing feels easy or familiar. We have to be intentional with every action and thought, making each choice with care. This new, deliberate way of being can feel uncomfortable, even artificial at times, like we're piecing together a new version of ourselves without knowing if it will truly fit.

Sometimes I even catch myself comparing my current choices to what an old version of me would've done. I'll think, "Well, three years ago I would have . . . ," and remember how I might have reacted in an unhealthy way, whether by self-sabotaging or maybe even shutting down completely and ghosting everyone who cared about me. I knew that past version of myself well; I was her for most of my life. And now, while I know I'm moving forward in a healthier way, there's a sense of loss that comes with it. It's surprisingly heavy to let go of an identity, even one that no longer serves us. Mourning who we used to be is natural, even when we know that change is for the better.

We have to give ourselves permission to grieve that loss. It might sound odd, because we're still here—we haven't gone anywhere physically. But the person we were—wild, codependent, self-deprecating, or whatever qualities defined our past self—is no longer the person we are becoming. It's okay to feel that sadness and acknowledge that loss. Grief isn't just for the death of people we love; it can be a part of any major life shift. We can grieve relationships that have ended, friendships with people who are still alive but no longer in our lives for good reasons, jobs or careers that didn't pan out, even dreams that we've outgrown. Loss is loss, and it deserves our time and compassion as we move forward.

EARNING IT

It's common to put off our happiness or growth, telling ourselves that we'll finally feel content and move on once we land that new job, make more money, or find the right relationship. We may feel like we must earn the right to get better. For many of us, myself included, our advancement and contentment seem contingent upon these external achievements. It's as if enjoying life isn't something everyone deserves by default, but rather something we have to toil and sweat for. Otherwise, it feels like we don't deserve it if we haven't struggled enough to truly earn our place or our happiness.

What's ironic is that even as I recognize this pattern in myself, believing that I'll be happy when this or that finally happens, I find myself looking at others who seem to have what I want and feeling jealous. It's as though they have access to something I don't, seemingly having a fast track to growth or happiness that I haven't quite reached yet. I look at them and think, "What am I missing? How did they get there so effortlessly?" In those moments it's important to remember that we all have the same potential for joy and change in our lives. The only real obstacle is our belief that we need to earn it or that we don't yet deserve to feel content until we've crossed some imaginary finish line.

Maybe we feel this way because change takes time. It's not something we can fast-track no matter how hard we try. It's a lot like trying to grow a plant (which I am not good at, by the way). You can water it, give it sunlight, and make sure the soil is right, but you can't rush the process of growing. Imagine standing over that plant every day and getting frustrated that it's not blooming fast enough. You water it more, move it to different spots, or even try to pull on the leaves to make it grow quicker. But all that extra effort doesn't help; in fact, it often harms the plant. What you can't see is the growth that is happening beneath the surface. The plant is changing at its own pace, and no matter how much you want to control it, you have to let it unfold naturally.

That's where the real challenge lies, not just in making changes but in accepting that growth is slow, and often invisible at first. It's about learning to sit with the discomfort of not seeing progress right away and trusting that the work we're doing is laying the foundation for something greater. It's hard to stay motivated when the results feel so far away, and it's natural to wish the process was easier or faster. But even though I sometimes hate the pace, I also know that meaningful, lasting change isn't supposed to be instant. It's a gradual unfolding, a slow rewiring of old patterns, and it takes time for that to really sink in and take hold.

If we did get immediate results, if everything we desired came to us in an instant, would we truly value them? Would we appreciate the effort, growth, and resilience that come from the journey, or would it all feel somewhat hollow? Instant gratification often diminishes the significance of our achievements because it bypasses the essential process of struggle, learning, and self-discovery.

Think about it: When we work hard for something, whether it's a personal goal, a career aspiration, or a meaningful relationship, the challenges we face along the way shape our character and deepen our understanding of ourselves and the world around us. The trials, setbacks, and moments of doubt not only teach us resilience but also allow us to cultivate gratitude for the eventual rewards. It's like working for things somehow increases their value.

I remember in college getting into a friend's new BMW and being shocked at how poorly they were taking care of it. There was trash on the floor, spilled coffee on the console, and makeup all over the dash. It was a mess. I asked if they wanted help cleaning it, but they brushed me off, saying their dad leased them a new car every year or so, so they didn't have to worry about it. They didn't care that this was a dream car for many people, or that owning any vehicle usually comes with a sense of pride and responsibility. They didn't care about it because they didn't work for it, and therefore it didn't have any value.

We can take things for granted when they come to us without effort or sacrifice. For my friend, the car was just another object, a temporary possession that didn't hold the same worth as it might for someone who had worked hard to earn it. When we don't invest personally, financially, or even emotionally in something, we are more likely to overlook its significance.

OVERLOOKING OURSELVES

It's true that if everything were handed to us, we might not fully grasp the value of those outcomes. They could feel more like fleeting moments rather than hard-earned milestones. However, the opposite can also hold us back. When we work hard for something but don't allow ourselves to appreciate what we've accomplished, we can get stuck in a cycle of constantly pushing for more without ever taking time to reflect or celebrate.

I know I work hard for the things I want, but I often have a hard time truly acknowledging the significance of my achievements. For example, when my first book came out, I was thrilled—but instead of taking a moment to celebrate, I immediately pushed myself to move on to the next project. I barely gave myself time to enjoy the fruits of my labor, and that's something many of us do. Even when we invest deeply, we can overlook our success.

I often feel uncomfortable acknowledging a win or celebrating something I've worked for. There's a part of me that fears if I do, I'll let my foot off the gas and lose everything I've worked so hard to achieve. It's as if I believe that unless I'm constantly producing or earning, I'm not safe or okay, like my worth is tied entirely to what I accomplish. It's the only way I've known to receive the love and attention I crave. If I'm not working hard, I feel worthless or, worse, like I'm in the way. Even as I write this, I realize it all goes back to my belief that love has to be earned. These issues run deep and make it difficult for me to acknowledge all of the areas in my life where I'm succeeding.

There's another layer to this too: Feeling good or proud of ourselves can feel dangerous. Many of us are afraid that if we acknowledge our accomplishments, it'll signal to others that we don't need help or support anymore. We may fear the isolation that could come along with that type of response. We can worry that if we do too well, we will lose out on certain relationships or care. We might also fear that celebrating ourselves will make us vulnerable to criticism or judgment. We could've been taught, through experience, that showing pride or joy can lead to someone tearing us down or making us feel small.

That's why we often avoid celebrating our successes. It can feel safer to stay quiet, to keep moving, and to avoid the potential pain. But this mindset keeps us stuck. We need to teach our nervous system, through repeated exposure, that it's okay to feel proud, happy, and excited. These emotions won't lead to rejection or harm. Instead, they'll build up our confidence and help us realize that it's safe to feel good about what we've accomplished. And the right people will want to celebrate our successes right along with us.

TRUSTING THE PROCESS

This part of the work is where I struggle the most, even flounder. I like things to feel under control, and when I just have to trust that it will turn out, that's when I start to falter. My instinct is to grasp tighter and to force things to happen. Letting go and trusting the process feels uncertain, risky, and out of my hands.

And yet this book is about control...and all the ways it holds us back. This is exactly what I need to relinquish. As we've explored so far—and as I've learned firsthand—my attempts to take control often backfire. Instead of moving things forward, I end up tangled in frustration and self-doubt, overthinking every step, second-guessing whether I'm even on the right path. The more I try to force certainty, the more stuck I become.

This is when my urge to give up is at its strongest. The tension I feel even talking about this part of the process is palpable. Going against my innate urge to pull, strain, and fight feels unnatural. I immediately find myself repeating the story of how without my constant controlling and pushing, I wouldn't be where I am today. That I can't relax or trust that it will just work out, because then my guard will be down, and bad things could happen. It could all fall apart and I will look stupid because I didn't do anything to try and stop it. When that story starts playing, I often feel that maybe it's best if I just decide to give up. That way I am in control of how it ends.

Self-sabotage is such a common urge during this "trusting" period because it's the last option we have when trying to control the outcome. I love the American version of *The Office*, and one of the characters, Andy Bernard, has a great quote for this very feeling. He says, "Andy Bernard does not lose contests. He wins them. Or he quits them because they're unfair." When we don't feel like we have any control over something, we can, often without realizing it, decide to just quit. I have done this many times. I will end relationships rather than have a difficult conversation, or claim that I don't really want to do something for which I have fought for years because it doesn't look like it's going to turn out.

In many ways, I would rather quit than risk facing the possibility of failure. The fear of things not going the way I envision can make "opting out" feel like the safer, easier choice. Self-sabotage in these moments feels like a form of control. If I end things myself, at least I'm the one steering the ship. But this impulse to quit or downplay what I truly want is a protective mechanism. By convincing myself I don't really care, I shield myself from disappointment. However, every time I choose to self-sabotage, I'm holding myself back not only from growth but also from the deeper, lasting fulfillment that comes with trusting the process, even when it's uncertain and messy. Learning to stay and engage, even when things are tough, is where real change begins.

SLIP-UPS

It's incredibly common to slip back into old habits and ways of thinking, especially when we're feeling overwhelmed, exhausted, or uncertain. After all, these patterns developed over time as ways to cope, to feel safe, and to keep life manageable. When we're faced with stress or doubt, it's natural to lean on what's familiar, even if it's no longer helpful. I think that's why we sometimes fall back into habits we've worked hard to break, like reaching back out to that toxic ex of ours or overcommitting to projects at work. These patterns may not be healthy, but they offer a sense of comfort and control that can feel reassuring in times of uncertainty.

Reverting to old ways doesn't erase our progress; it just highlights where we're still learning and healing. Each slip-up is an opportunity to gain insight into what we need at that moment. Maybe it's rest, maybe reassurance, or maybe just a reminder to breathe and regroup. Recognizing these needs, and the triggers that send us into those old patterns, is the first step in breaking free from them. We often think of setbacks as failures, but they're checkpoints where we can pause, reflect, and refocus.

Over time, these moments become powerful turning points. Each time we catch ourselves falling back into our old routines, we're building self-awareness and, more importantly, self-compassion. By understanding why we return to certain habits, we empower ourselves to make different choices in the future. It's this awareness that ultimately strengthens our resilience and keeps us moving forward.

Progress isn't always a straight line. It's more like a winding road, with twists, turns, and the occasional backtrack. When we view setbacks as part of the process rather than as failures, we let go of perfection and make room for genuine growth. It's about accepting that real change takes time, patience, and the willingness to forgive ourselves when things don't go perfectly. Each time we slip and then choose to realign, we're proving that, even with setbacks, we're still moving forward—slowly, steadily, and more self-aware with each step.

It's a process, not perfection.

THE NEXT STEP

The power of change isn't in sweeping gestures or instant transformations. It's in the quiet moments, in the small, intentional shifts we can make to loosen that tether, even if only by an inch. Maybe growth is found in the daily decision to try again, to take one small step toward something different, even if it's as simple as showing up for ourselves in a way we haven't before. It could be keeping a promise to ourselves or picking a small way to put ourselves first, prioritizing our own growth over others' expectations.

When we don't know what to do or what our next step should be, maybe that's not as daunting as it seems. We could see it as an exciting time, a moment when we are actually at our freest to choose a new path or a new way. As daunting as it feels, there's a kind of freedom on the other side of change. By letting go of the need for perfection or control, we give ourselves room to make progress, however slow or messy it might be.

Even though I'm not there yet, I'm learning to trust that feeling stuck doesn't mean I'm failing. I'm choosing to see it as a time for me to gather the strength to continue doing the hard work of change. I think that's the real journey: the courage to keep moving, even when we don't know where the path will lead, and trusting in ourselves to travel that path without controlling every step. As we keep moving, more of the path will reveal itself, just like we drive a winding dark road at night and the headlights light up more of the way as we go.

Change may not come easily or feel comfortable, but it's where new possibilities start. It's also necessary if we want to continue to grow. While it can be challenging to keep our motivation to try and we may sometimes allow our thoughts to keep us stuck, if we can sit with the discomfort and let go of our need for control, we might just find that we're more capable of moving forward than we ever thought.

"WHY DO I KEEP DOING THIS?" EXERCISE— *QUESTIONS TO BETTER UNDERSTAND AND MANAGE FEELING DEPRESSED AND STUCK*

1. In what areas of your life do you feel the most resistance to change, and why do you think that is?
2. Which fear of change resonated with you most in this chapter? Why do you think that is?
3. How do you typically respond to feelings of uncertainty or discomfort? Are those responses helping or hindering your growth?
4. What small, intentional shift can you make today to begin loosening the tether of feeling stuck?

5. When was the last time you embraced a moment of uncertainty as an opportunity for growth? What did you learn from that experience?
6. How can you practice self-compassion when you find yourself slipping back into old habits?
7. What does it mean to you to trust the process of change, and how can you cultivate that trust in your life?

CONTROL CHALLENGE

For the next week, challenge yourself to **actively celebrate** your accomplishments—big or small—and notice how your body reacts. Since control often shows up in how we manage our emotions and responses, this exercise will help loosen the grip of self-protection and allow you to experience pride, happiness, and excitement without shutting them down.

Steps to Complete the Challenge

Identify three wins daily: Each day, write down three things you're proud of, no matter how small. Maybe you spoke up in a meeting, finished a book, or resisted the urge to downplay a compliment.

Share a success: Tell a trusted friend or partner, or even post online (if you're comfortable) about something you're proud of. Notice how you feel before, during, and after sharing.

Practice sitting with positive emotions: When you feel happiness, pride, or excitement, pause. Breathe. Let yourself sit with it for at least thirty seconds instead of brushing it off or minimizing it.

Observe your reactions to praise: Pay attention to how you respond when someone acknowledges your success. Do you deflect, downplay, or accept it fully? Try simply saying, "Thank you," and letting the compliment land.

Reflect on the experience: At the end of the week, ask yourself:

- "Did I feel resistance to celebrating myself?"
- "How did my nervous system react (discomfort, ease, excitement)?"
- "What changed when I allowed myself to embrace my accomplishments?"

This challenge will help retrain your nervous system to see **joy, pride, and success as safe emotions**—ones that don't need to be controlled, hidden, or downplayed.

Chapter 11

LEARNING TO LET GO

Making the Decision to Stop Fighting Ourselves

LETTING GO HAS ALWAYS FELT LIKE GIVING UP. TO ME, IF I'M NOT actively fighting for something, it signals that I don't want it badly enough or that it's not worth pursuing. Phrases like "trust the process" or "let go and let God" have always felt frustratingly passive, as if they're asking me to surrender any influence I have over my own life. It's hard to accept the idea of standing back and trusting that things will work out on their own, especially when I've convinced myself that it's never too late to change or control an outcome. I just have to try harder.

This way of thinking has been with me my entire life. I hold on to things I can't control, clinging to the idea that if I control my efforts, then I can shift the outcome. But deep down, I know it doesn't work like that. What's worse is that this tendency shows up in subtle but destructive ways: passive aggression, intense anxiety that spills over into how I treat others, and an overall intensity that I don't like about myself. I try to mask it with a calm, capable exterior, but the inner need for control is always lurking, draining my energy and pulling me into a cycle of frustration and guilt.

I recently saw a meme that said, "Me saying that I have let it go," alongside a drawing of an octopus holding on to something with a few of its tentacles while lifting the others in the air as if pretending they weren't attached. It was funny and incredibly relatable. It helped me realize how often I convince myself I've let go, when in reality I'm still clinging to something with just enough grip to feel in control.

I think we all do this. We tell ourselves we've let go of a relationship, a past mistake, or an unfulfilled dream, but we still cling to some piece of it. Maybe it's the hope that we can still steer things toward a different outcome or the fear of facing that we truly have no control over how things turn out. Holding on to these illusions of control can feel comforting, like we're keeping a grip on something that's slipping away, but in the end, it only keeps us stuck. We miss out on the freedom that comes with surrender, the peace that comes with truly moving forward.

For me, this need to control and hold on boils down to a fear of vulnerability. If I let go completely, I risk feeling exposed, left to face disappointment or hurt without a shield. Keeping a few tentacles around the things I care about makes me feel as though I can prevent pain, as though my efforts can somehow guarantee a favorable outcome. Letting go, in my mind, feels like stepping into harm's way; it's as if I'm removing all protection, leaving myself open to the worst.

INTERNAL CHAOS

The irony, though, is that this desire for control creates more chaos than calm, as we've learned over the course of this book. While I hold on, trying to manage things I have no power over, I become tense, anxious, and easily triggered. The price I pay for this false sense of control is high: It disrupts my peace, strains my relationships, and keeps me constantly on edge. From the outside, I can look calm and happy, but internally I feel like a beehive humming with thoughts, worries, and the urge to take action when things feel slightly out of my control. It's like a constant, buzzing need to fix, adjust, or prepare for every possible outcome, even when I know it's impossible to cover every angle. The outer calm hides an inner storm, one where I'm always bracing, anticipating, and trying to hold things together.

I saw this internal struggle play out just this morning while waiting for my yearly dermatologist checkup. The woman sitting next to me had already been there when I arrived. After about fifteen minutes, she got up to check with the front desk, asking how much longer it would be since she'd already been waiting over thirty minutes. They assured her it wouldn't be much longer, so she returned to her seat beside me.

As more time passed without her name being called, her frustration became palpable. She began crossing and uncrossing her legs so forcefully that the couch we were sharing started to shake. At one point, she jumped up as if jolted, only to sit back down heavily. She sighed loudly, flipped her hair, and continued fidgeting restlessly. Finally, she got up again to check with the front desk. Her anxiety was so intense it felt like it was spilling out of her and into the entire waiting room, including my own space. I felt relieved when they finally called her name, uncertain what she might do if the wait had continued any longer.

She had no control over how late the doctor was running but was doing everything in her power to try and speed her appointment up, to control the outcome. For her, letting go, relaxing, and submitting to the process seemed impossible. While I don't know her situation, and she could have been late for work or school, I do know that she created the chaos all on her own. She made an appointment for a time and didn't give herself any wiggle room, and when things ran late, she couldn't tolerate the unpredictability. She could have told them she couldn't wait and would have to reschedule, but instead she let the anxiety build, causing herself and everyone around her discomfort.

If I had spoken up and told this woman to just relax, that everything would be okay, and to stop trying to control things beyond her grasp, she probably would have yelled at me—and rightly so. But the truth is that we all make choices like this every day. We don't give ourselves enough time to do something and we stress about how long it's taking. We don't communicate our expectations clearly and are then let down when they aren't met. We insist on doing it all ourselves because we want to have full control, and then we are burned out and mad no one helped. In many ways, we cling to things beyond our control and then feel frustrated when we realize we can't control them. This desire to control our surroundings often highlights just how little control we truly have. It's like we inadvertently trigger ourselves.

CURRENT DEFINITIONS

Since it's common for us to accidentally sabotage our efforts to let go, we will have to approach this creatively. Simply learning to breathe and "trust the process" may leave us like that octopus, holding on while pretending we aren't. We have to dive deeper into our beliefs about letting go, as our definitions may not be entirely accurate. Often, we cling to outdated definitions that suggest letting go is dangerous or painful, but that isn't the case. To truly move forward, we don't just need to learn to let go; we need to redefine what letting go means to us.

The interesting thing about working on myself while also being a therapist is that occasionally I manage to successfully apply what I teach to my own life. One of my go-to tools as a therapist is helping patients get clear on their definitions of terms, goals, and even their own beliefs. This clarity ensures we're on the same page and, more importantly, reveals areas where our definitions might be limiting us or holding us back. In my case, I define letting go as giving up, but that definition doesn't quite line up. If I want to have any chance of making a positive change in my life, I am going to have to challenge the way I think about letting go and come up with a new, more correct definition.

This doesn't mean I need to consult Merriam-Webster's Dictionary. While it would provide a clear, textbook definition, that's not what I'm after. My goal is to understand why I connect these two words so closely and to tease apart their differences in a way that feels meaningful and helpful to me. Definitions on paper are valuable, but they're often removed from the nuances of personal experience.

I realize this approach might make some of my inner "fact-checkers" uncomfortable because it challenges the idea of an absolute, "correct" definition. However, in the therapeutic world, accuracy isn't always the priority; instead, it's often about helping people feel seen, heard, and understood. Defining things for ourselves is part of that process. It's less about rigid correctness and more about finding a framework that resonates with our inner experiences, which can help us navigate life in a way that feels authentic and empowering. When we redefine concepts personally, we create meanings that allow us to move forward with clarity, even if the definitions don't match a dictionary's precision.

Letting go means releasing something or loosening your grip on it. I envision it as setting a bird free from its cage or opening a gate to let cows roam free. This imagery evokes a sense of freedom, yet I still associate letting go with giving up. Why is that?

Perhaps it's because letting go signifies relinquishing my false sense of control, or it might stem from the belief that not containing something suggests I don't care about its outcome. I fear that if I release it, I'll lose it entirely, leading to pain or regret. Additionally, I might associate letting go with abandonment, as if I'm leaving something behind rather than allowing it to thrive in its own space.

REDEFINING

As I write this, I realize that I equate letting go with leaving things behind, and it dawns on me that this belief might be part of what keeps me holding on so tightly. I feel that to let something go, I must strip away my attachment to it, stop caring, and accept that it might not return. This notion has always made letting go feel harsh and final, almost like giving up. For goals and projects, I tell myself I can let go only if my emotional investment has faded. In relationships, my grip is even tighter; I want to hold on because that's how I've learned to show care. To let go feels like saying, "I don't care about this anymore," or "I've given up on this."

But maybe it doesn't have to mean that. Maybe letting go doesn't have to be a process of detachment, where we pull away from things that matter to us. What if letting go could be redefined as releasing our need to control how things turn out, trusting that they'll unfold in ways we may not predict? Letting go might not mean we care less; it could mean we trust more. It could mean we stop gripping so tightly because we trust that we'll be okay no matter the outcome.

This shift in perspective allows us to remain connected to our dreams, projects, and relationships without feeling chained to a specific outcome. We don't have to lose interest or stop caring; instead, we might just need to release the pressure we place on ourselves to make things go a certain way. Letting go could mean being open to different possibilities, allowing room for things to change or evolve in ways we can't control.

This redefinition challenges the belief that control equals care. It invites us to care deeply without needing to orchestrate every detail and to be present without needing guarantees. Ultimately, this approach to letting go can be liberating. It gives us permission to invest in what matters to us yet frees us from the weight of expecting specific outcomes. It allows us to stay connected, grounded, and open to growth, even as we relinquish our tight grasp on what comes next.

This reframing allows us to see letting go as an act of courage, not detachment. We're saying, "I trust that whatever happens, I'll be okay." It can be a way of showing respect for our resilience, our ability to adapt, and our willingness to let life unfold, even if it's not exactly as we planned.

IMPERFECTION

This process isn't going to be easy or perfect. It's not like we can suddenly understand something and a switch has been flipped. We have to meet ourselves where we are. I think this point is often missed when we aim for lasting change. We might want to jump ahead, pretending we never struggled with control, almost as if we're changing for a version of ourselves that doesn't exist. It's like those memes that say, "I set two alarms each morning: one for the person I wish I was, and another for who I truly am." Real change has to come from who we are right now, not who we imagine we could be. We're laying the foundation for that future self, but each step has to meet us where we are today. Only by accepting ourselves in the present can we build a path toward that new version, one step at a time.

When we embrace this approach, we release ourselves from the pressure to do things flawlessly. The process of change *will* be imperfect and messy, because growth requires us to test, stumble, and adjust along the way. It's a bit like learning to walk. You don't start by running; you start by taking uncertain, unsteady steps. This approach might feel counterintuitive, especially if we're used to forcing ourselves into a mold of who we think we should be, but fighting against our true selves is exhausting. Constantly striving to "fix" ourselves can actually reinforce a cycle of resistance and make the process harder and longer than it needs to be.

This is why I believe the path of least resistance is often the most powerful path to change. When we stop fighting ourselves and start working with what's already here, we open the door to real, compassionate growth. This doesn't mean we're settling for less or abandoning our goals; it means we're working with our natural strengths, tendencies, and even flaws. It's important to note that the least resistance does not equate to easy or the most comfortable. It simply means that we aren't trying to force something that's not meant to be.

When we work with our reality instead of against it, we can stop wasting energy on what isn't possible, like trying to control someone else's actions or insisting on doing everything ourselves at work or school when we know collaboration could improve the outcome. By releasing these uphill struggles, we create space to grow in ways that resonate with us, building resilience and progress that's sustainable. This approach isn't about taking shortcuts; it's about moving forward in a way that respects who we are now while guiding us toward who we want to become.

In my case, this means I have to slowly loosen my grip on control. If that means leaving a small "window open" so I still feel like I can take it back if needed, then that's okay. I'm learning to work with, not against, myself. Progress doesn't require me to abandon who I am entirely; it just asks me to trust that I can move forward without holding everything so tightly. By making room for flexibility, I can find a healthier balance, one that allows growth without losing the comfort of feeling grounded along the way.

ASSUAGING FEARS

We hold on so tightly to control because it feels safer. Clinging to what we know creates an illusion of stability, as if we can guard ourselves against uncertainty, disappointment, or loss. But to truly let go and allow life to flourish, we need to feel secure enough to loosen our grip. This means understanding what control seems to offer us and finding healthier ways to meet those needs.

For me, control creates a sense of stability, connection, and security, as if I can predict outcomes and shield myself from pain. But I'm beginning to see that this is just an illusion. Control doesn't provide any of those things. In reality, the need to control can limit me, keeping me in a state of resistance rather than openness. By trying to manage every outcome, I end up stifling my growth, as well as the growth of those around me. I feel more anxious, less sure of myself and my relationships, and more isolated than ever before. I'm realizing that control doesn't give me what I'm looking for; it only takes away, demanding constant energy and attention without ever truly delivering the comfort or certainty it promises. It's like I am working hard to fill a pitcher with water without realizing there's a hole in the bottom.

The hard truth is that holding on doesn't protect me from pain; it only prolongs it. The more I cling to control, the more I deprive myself of true stability, connection, and security. Instead of trying to control everything, I can start building real support in other ways: by learning to trust myself, prioritizing my well-being so I'm less reactive and less tempted to micromanage, and investing in relationships that bring genuine connection. These sources of security don't demand constant effort to maintain. They provide a deeper, lasting sense of peace. Letting go of control, then, becomes an act of self-trust, opening up space for growth and a more authentic sense of safety that I don't have to work so hard to maintain.

LIFE'S GOT MY BACK

Self-trust is something I've worked on for years, and it's been a challenging but incredibly rewarding journey. In my twenties, I vividly remember how much I relied on the validation of others. I constantly sought reassurance from those around me, convinced that their approval would somehow confirm my worth or guide me in the right direction. Looking back, I feel a twinge of embarrassment at how much power I handed over to others, rather than trusting myself.

Over time, though, I've come to see a pattern that keeps me grounded when I start to doubt my next move: Every single time I've trusted my gut, it has worked out.

Every. Single. Time.

It's taken years to realize that I truly know what's right and wrong for me. I understand my limits, what I can handle, and what I need to say no to, even when those choices don't align with others' expectations.

For those who've had a rougher path, though, this journey may look and feel different. Sometimes, life hasn't always seemed to "work out," and trusting oneself can feel like stepping onto shaky ground. It can be especially hard to hear or believe in your inner voice when past experiences have left scars or eroded your confidence in making decisions. For many, learning to trust yourself may be about taking small, gentle steps toward your intuition—noticing when that knot in your stomach is trying to tell you, "This isn't good for you," or recognizing that you feel more energized and lighter when you're around certain people or doing certain things.

Self-trust doesn't have to mean having all the answers. It can start with simply acknowledging these small signals that guide you, even if they don't always feel clear at first. Over time, as you pay attention to these cues, you might find that your intuition gets a little stronger and a little more reliable. Trusting yourself can mean being patient and compassionate as you navigate this path, especially if your life has been filled with times when your voice was drowned out by others' opinions or judgments, or even your self-doubt.

Sometimes, it's less about knowing exactly what to do and more about building a sense of safety within yourself, trusting that even if things don't go perfectly, you have the strength to handle it. Reconnecting with your intuition could be as simple as taking time each day to check in with how you feel, journaling your thoughts without censoring yourself, or taking a few moments of stillness to see what's really on your mind.

And as you start to tune in, you might begin to notice patterns: things that reliably make you feel at peace, environments where you feel relaxed, people who bring out the best in you. These small insights can serve as guideposts, gently leading you toward decisions that align with your true self, even if that voice feels faint right now. With time, the process of listening and responding to your intuition becomes a pathway to self-trust, a kind of inner stability that isn't shaken by the opinions of others or the uncertainty of life. It becomes a quiet but steady foundation, reminding you that even if life's path is winding, you have a place of clarity within you that you can rely on.

Learning to trust myself in this way has been one of my most valuable lessons. I've realized that even when things are hard, I can find my way through. In fact, there's never been a time when I couldn't figure it out. Now I know I can rely on myself, and I can hear my inner voice when I quiet the noise around me.

Self-trust isn't about having all the answers up front or feeling certain every step of the way. It's about trusting that I can navigate whatever comes, knowing that I'm resilient and capable. I just have to listen closely and lean into that quiet confidence, letting it guide me forward one decision at a time.

BUILDING TRUST

Trusting ourselves takes time and effort. I am not going to lie to you and say that you can do this in three easy steps, but there are small practices we can integrate into our daily lives that make all the difference.

The first and most important step is that we have to spend time with ourselves. How can we trust someone we don't know? We can't. We have to learn to be okay with being alone, listening to our thoughts, noticing how our body feels. I know this isn't easy or comfortable, but that's the point. Change doesn't happen when we stay in our comfort zone. It happens when we push ourselves to think and act differently.

My favorite way of spending quality time with myself is to journal. I know I keep mentioning this, but it's because I am hoping you will pick up on the hints and give it a try. I love to ask myself questions, check my facts, and ponder the reasons I am thinking or feeling a certain way. Journaling gives me the space I need to sort through all that's going on inside of me. When I put my thoughts on paper, I gain clarity; I can spot patterns, understand why I react the way I do, and see where I can choose differently. Journaling helps me connect with who I am today, and it allows me to envision who I'd like to become tomorrow.

Next, I love to go for walks. No podcast on, no music in my earbuds, just me and my thoughts. Something about the movement seems to help me emotionally move through things more quickly. It also means I am away from home, so there aren't as many distractions from myself. While I was writing my last two books I would take myself on long walks every afternoon. It helped me put certain thoughts together, figure out where I wanted to take a chapter, or recall a personal story to illustrate a point.

Walking has a way of clearing my mind and allowing ideas to flow more freely. As my body moves, my thoughts seem to fall into rhythm with each step, creating space for reflection that sitting at a desk or staring at a screen simply can't offer. These walks give me the mental clarity to see things from a fresh perspective. Often, I return with a new direction or a solution I hadn't thought of before. It's also during these walks that I will realize I've neglected a boundary, fallen into old habits, or need to communicate my expectations more clearly. It's amazing how something so simple can help untangle the mess of thoughts and emotions that accumulate throughout the day. Plus, being outside in nature, even for just a short time, is grounding. It's a reminder that there's a bigger picture beyond my day-to-day concerns.

Spending intentional time alone in these ways fosters a relationship with ourselves that, over time, becomes one of trust. The more I show up for myself, the more I realize I can count on myself. And here's the surprising part: When we trust ourselves, we're less afraid of the unknown because we know we have our own back. We no longer need to control everything around us to feel safe; we can be grounded within ourselves.

These small steps help us become friends with ourselves, encouraging kindness and patience along the way. Bit by bit, we start to see that we're capable of handling whatever comes our way. Self-trust isn't about perfection or certainty. It's about knowing we can face life, however messy, and navigate it one step at a time. The more we practice this, the more we open ourselves up to real, lasting change. It may not be easy, but it's the most authentic, sustainable journey we can take.

IS THAT REALLY PROGRESS?

Real, lasting change rarely mirrors the idealized, polished version we see in our minds. We often picture success as a linear progression: one clear step after another, each moment marked by a visible leap forward. But true transformation doesn't always unfold in such a tidy, predictable way. Instead, it's often messy, nonlinear, and full of unexpected detours.

When we set out to change something in our lives, whether it's building better habits, healing from past pain, or letting go of old behaviors, we often expect instant progress. We want to see results right away, and if we don't, we might start to doubt ourselves. But the truth is that real change takes time, and it's rarely a smooth, straight line. We need to check in on how we are defining progress, and if it's realistic or not.

Think about that friend you haven't seen in ten years. The changes are probably obvious right away. Her hair is different, she might dress in a way you don't remember, her accent is gone, and now she's a mom. Each of those changes happened gradually over time, through decisions she made and experiences she lived. The same is true for you, but because you see yourself every day, the changes are subtle and harder to spot. It can feel like you need a magnifying glass to notice them, but they're there. Growth happens slowly, and even when it feels like nothing's shifting, you're still evolving. Trust that, like your friend, you're growing and changing, even if it's not always obvious from day to day.

Progress isn't always about taking huge leaps. Often, it's the small, authentic steps that make all the difference. Maybe one day you manage to set a healthy boundary, and the next you slip up, but each time you practice, you're moving forward. Maybe you don't change your habits overnight, but you make one better choice today than you did yesterday. These small victories are the foundation of lasting change, even if they don't feel monumental at the time.

You're not in competition with anyone else; you're only competing with your past self. Every time you make a better choice, even in a small way, you're moving forward. It might not feel like much, but those little victories add up over time, and before you know it, you'll be amazed at how far you've come. Whenever one of my patients is feeling stuck or unmotivated I offer to read them my notes from one of our sessions six months ago. The drastic changes they see usually shock them, and even if they don't say it, I know they feel proud of themselves. We can get so caught up in the here and now that we lose sight of how far we have come. If you aren't in therapy right now, you can look back on your journal entries from a few months ago to get the same effect. I promise you'll see a shift, even if it feels subtle.

So, trust yourself. Let go of the pressure to change overnight. The truth is that sustainable growth happens when you stop rushing and give yourself the grace to take things one step at a time. You're already on the path. Keep going, because each small step is shaping the person you're becoming, and that person is more capable, more resilient, and more amazing than you realize. You're doing the work. You've got this.

WE ALWAYS BOUNCE BACK

As you continue on your journey of change, remember this: Life has an incredible way of unfolding, even when we can't see exactly how it will all come together. It's easy to get caught up in the belief that if things don't look perfect or follow a clear path, we're doing something wrong. But life isn't rigid, and neither is growth. The most meaningful transformations often come in unexpected ways, when we allow ourselves the space to adapt and learn along the way.

You have the strength within you to navigate the uncertainty and challenges that arise. It might not always be clear where the road is headed, and it may feel like you're walking through fog, but trust that the resilience to adapt is already within you. Each step forward, no matter how uncertain, is still progress. You've weathered storms before, and you will again. This moment of uncertainty? It's just another chapter of the story you're writing.

Letting go of the need for control doesn't mean you're losing your way. On the contrary, it creates the space for new experiences, insights, and growth that you might not even be able to imagine right now. It's in that openness, that willingness to let things unfold, where true transformation can happen.

I often reflect on my life and career, and I never in my wildest dreams thought I would be creating videos online or have the privilege of writing books! I had no idea where my life would take me, and if I had fought against it, clinging to control and avoiding any risk, it might not have turned out this way. And to be honest, I can't imagine it any other way now. Letting go of the need to control every detail has opened up so many unexpected opportunities and experiences that I wouldn't have had if I stayed locked in fear. It's a reminder that sometimes the most fulfilling paths are the ones we never saw coming.

When you stop trying to force everything into a neat, predictable mold, you start to see that change is not about following a strict plan, but about trusting yourself to handle whatever comes. The small, flexible actions you take every day are what build the foundation for sustainable, lasting change. Trust that you are capable of adapting, learning, and growing, no matter how messy or nonlinear the journey may seem. You are stronger and more resilient than you think, and the path you're on is exactly where you need to be.

As long as you continue to trust yourself, stay open to growth, and embrace the journey as it unfolds, you'll find that the life you're creating for yourself is far richer and more rewarding than anything you could have planned. Let go of the need to control every detail, and trust that life's resilience will carry you forward. Keep going. The best parts of your story are still ahead.

FREEDOM

Imagine you're a bird who has been trapped in a small, confined space for years. You're constantly aware of the walls closing in, your every movement restricted, your breath shallow. You've fought to get out, tried to pry open the bars, but no matter how hard you try, the cage remains locked. Now picture the moment when, without warning, the door swings open. You feel the cool breeze against your feathers, the vast expanse of the sky, and the weight of the cage lifting off you. Suddenly, you're free. You can fly.

This is what it feels like when we let go of that constant struggle for control. When we stop fighting against ourselves, against life, against every little thing that doesn't fit our rigid plans, it's a kind of freedom we didn't know was possible. We realize, for the first time, that life will be okay. We will be okay. Things will work out. The fight we thought we needed to win wasn't really a fight at all, it was just resistance to something bigger, something more expansive, something lighter.

When we hold on so tightly to control, we're like that bird in the cage. We think we need to force our way out, manipulate our surroundings, and bend everything to our will. But what if the freedom we crave isn't something we fight for, but something we allow? What if we simply open our hands, let go, and trust that the door will open when it's time? What if, instead of swimming against the current, we lean into the flow of it?

Letting go doesn't mean giving up. It doesn't mean surrendering to chaos or losing direction. It means we stop trying to force everything into our idea of how it should be. It's like letting go of the grip we've had on the wheel for so long and realizing that the car is still driving just fine. It's driving better because we aren't white-knuckling every turn.

When we stop fighting the current, we begin to feel the freedom in it. We feel lighter. We can breathe deeper. The air feels fresher, the world feels bigger. We stop seeing every bump in the road as an obstacle and start seeing it as part of the journey. Instead of seeing ourselves as failures for not meeting our expectations, we see the beauty in the process, the way life unfolds in unpredictable, messy, yet perfect ways.

You don't need to keep fighting yourself. You don't need to keep proving that you're strong enough, capable enough, or in control. You are. You already are. You've been fighting against the flow of life for so long that it's hard to remember what freedom feels like. But when you stop gripping, when you let go of that need for perfection, when you release the hold you have on controlling everything, that's when you feel the wind on your skin. That's when you realize that freedom isn't about being perfect; it's about being present. It's about trusting the journey, trusting that things will work out, and knowing that you will be okay no matter what.

This is your invitation to stop. Stop fighting, stop forcing, stop overthinking. Lean into the freedom that is already there, just waiting for you to open your eyes to it. The next time you feel the urge to control, to grasp at something you think you need, pause. Feel the wind. Know that you don't need to keep doing this. You can choose differently. You can choose freedom.

And when you do, life will feel lighter, your steps will feel freer, and you'll remember what it feels like to soar.

"WHY DO I KEEP DOING THIS ?" EXERCISE— *QUESTIONS TO HELP US STOP FIGHTING OURSELVES AND LEARN TO LET GO*

1. How do you define "letting go" and how does it feel to do it?
2. Have you ever experienced a time when "fighting" for what you wanted led to burnout or frustration? What happened?
3. How do you feel when you try to let go of control in a situation? What fears or discomforts arise, and why?
4. In what areas of your life do you feel the need to suffer or push through to succeed? How might this belief be limiting your growth and well-being?
5. When you reflect on your past struggles, what were the moments when things shifted, not because of control, but because of surrender or letting go?
6. What role does fear play in your desire for control, and how can you gently confront that fear to embrace the unknown?

CONTROL CHALLENGE

For the next **forty-eight hours**, practice **conscious surrender** in small but meaningful ways. Instead of forcing outcomes, overplanning, or trying to control situations, take a step back and let events unfold naturally.

Pick One Area to Release Control

Choose a specific situation where you tend to overcontrol. Some examples:

- Let someone else plan the details of an outing, dinner, or meeting without your input.

- Resist the urge to correct or "fix" something that isn't being done exactly how you'd do it.
- Allow a conversation to flow without rehearsing what you'll say in advance.
- Leave space in your schedule instead of filling every moment with tasks.

Set an Intention

Before stepping into the situation, take a deep breath and remind yourself: "I am choosing to trust this moment as it unfolds. I don't have to control everything for it to be okay."

Observe Your Reactions

Pay attention to what happens internally when you loosen your grip.

- Do you feel anxious, restless, or uncomfortable?
- What thoughts come up? ("If I don't step in, it will fall apart." "They'll think I'm not trying.")
- Where do you feel it in your body?

Reflect on the Outcome

After the experience, ask yourself:

- "Did things actually go wrong, or just not *my* way?"
- "What surprised me?"
- "How did it feel to let go, even for a little while?"

Write It Down

Jot down a quick reflection—just a few sentences—on what you noticed. If it was hard, that's okay. If it felt freeing, note that too.

Why This Matters

This exercise helps rewire your nervous system to see that surrendering control doesn't mean failure. It allows space for trust, flexibility, and even relief. True growth often happens **not when we grip tighter, but when we loosen our hold**.

Conclusion

As you close the pages of this book, I want to remind you that the story doesn't end here. In fact, it's just the beginning of something deeper, something more alive. We've talked a lot about control: how we fight to hold on, to try and shape the world around us into something manageable, predictable. But here's the truth: No matter how hard we try, control is an illusion. It's a dance, not a battle. And sometimes, the most powerful thing we can do is learn to let go.

Letting go doesn't mean giving up or abandoning your goals. It doesn't mean losing yourself in the chaos or sitting back passively while the world spins on. Letting go means creating space. Space for change, for growth, for unexpected opportunities. It's about trusting that you are already capable, strong, and enough. Even when things don't unfold the way you imagined.

I want you to remember this: The fight for control is not a battle you're meant to win. It's an invitation to evolve. It's the tension that teaches you what matters, what you're capable of, and what you're ready to release. And with each breath you take, you'll find yourself stepping into a new rhythm, one where you're no longer trying to micromanage every move, but instead trusting the process, even in the messiness of it all.

Change isn't something that happens overnight, and growth isn't always linear. But it is real, and it is happening, one moment, one choice at a time. Every time you show up for yourself, whether that's pushing through the hard days or giving yourself grace on the days that don't go as planned, you're moving forward. Every time you let go of a little bit of control, you're making room for something even better to come in.

You are not alone in this. We're all figuring it out together, one step at a time. Keep trusting yourself. Keep moving forward. And above all, keep remembering that it's not about being perfect, it's about being present. So, take a deep breath, let go, and trust that you are exactly where you need to be.

Tomorrow, you will be a little bit different. A little bit more free. And that's more than enough.

ACKNOWLEDGMENTS

First and foremost, thank you to my husband, Sean. Thank you for always believing in me, even when I struggle to believe in myself. Your calm, consistent, and unwavering love means everything to me. I'm grateful every day for meeting you when I did, and for the way you've loved every version of me over the past seventeen years, supporting my need to change and grow. None of this would have been possible without you and your support.

To my mom, my biggest cheerleader, thank you for always checking in, reminding me not to work too hard, and raising me to believe that the sky's the limit. It takes a strong woman to raise one, and I'm proud to come from a long line of them.

JL, you were the first to join my team when I was just a small mental health channel with a big dream. You believed in me, shared my vision, and fought to bring these books to life. I'll never forget all those meetings where we were told to shift the message, make it more palatable for a larger audience, or tailor it to the self-help crowd. But you didn't falter. Instead, we kept moving forward until we found an editor and publisher who truly understood our message. I feel so fortunate to have you as my literary agent and even luckier to call you my friend.

Linnea, the beginning of our partnership will always be etched in my memory: Yosemite, cooking over a fire pit, watching others dig trenches to manage the rain, and laughing until our stomachs hurt. You've always supported me, guided me when I was unsure of my next steps, and stayed consistent when I needed it most. Thank you for believing in me and for being such a wonderful manager and friend.

Harriet, I will forever be grateful that we were paired together just a few months before my first book, *Are u ok?*, came out. We hit it off right away, and you immediately jumped in—working hard, pushing to get me on podcasts and local news, and quoted in various blogs. Thank you for believing in me, for always having a vision of what we could accomplish, and for encouraging me to try new things. You are an amazing publicist and an even better friend.

Ellie, I'm so grateful that Mindy and Shaun connected us all those years ago. Thank you for always having my back, for answering all my odd questions, and for being the badass you are. I'm so glad we finally got to spend some nonwork time together last year, and I look forward to more yoga classes with you in the future!

Fabienne, thank you for agreeing to work with me. I know you like to keep things fresh and move around, but I'm so grateful that you've always stayed in my orbit. Without your support, insights, and assistance, none of this would be possible. You made it possible for me to carve out the time I needed for this book, and I'm deeply indebted to you for that.

Jared, I will always be thankful that YouTube connected us all those years ago. Thank you for choosing to work with me and for helping to bring my thoughts and ideas to life. Your guidance, insights, and unwavering support mean the world to me. I'm lucky to have you on this journey and so appreciative of everything you do.

Dan, none of this would be possible without you. Thank you for believing in my vision and recognizing the importance of bringing books like mine into the world. JL and I always called you "Dan the Man"—not only because you were the only man on our team at the time but also because you were incredible at what you did. Working with you on my first two books was such a pleasure, and I was truly saddened not to be able to finish this book with you. You have always been a trusted guide and champion for my work, and I'm so grateful for everything you've done.

Diana, jumping into a book project midway has to be tricky, but you did it effortlessly. Thank you for believing in me and in this book, and for understanding why it needed to be written. Your excitement and support have been invaluable, and I'm so grateful for the energy and dedication you brought to every step of the process. I couldn't have done it without you.

To everyone at Hachette and the many imprints within it that I've had the privilege to work with over the years, thank you for your invaluable guidance, constant encouragement, and dedication throughout the publishing process. Your expertise and commitment have been instrumental in bringing my work to life, and I'm deeply grateful for all you've contributed along the way.

Finally, to the members of my community, thank you for your unwavering support, for sharing your stories so openly, and for making all of this possible. I never imagined that my work would resonate so deeply with so many of you. Your courage, vulnerability, and kindness inspire me every day, and I feel truly honored to be a part of your journeys. Thank you for allowing me to do what I love and for helping create a space where we can all feel seen, heard, and understood.

NOTES

Chapter 2: Perfectionism and Feeling Like You're Not Enough

1. Julia Cameron, *The Artist's Way: A Spiritual Path to Higher Creativity* (New York: Putnam, 1992).
2. George Santayana, *The Life of Reason* (1905).

Chapter 3: People-Pleasing, Anxiety, and Manipulation

1. Salvador Minuchin, *Families and Family Therapy* (Cambridge, MA: Harvard University Press, 1974).

Chapter 5: Empathy and Being Overly Sensitive

1. Elaine Aron, *The Highly Sensitive Person: How to Thrive When the World Overwhelms You* (New York: Three Rivers Press, 1998).

Chapter 6: Numbing Out and Disconnecting

1. Paulo Coelho, *Veronika Decides to Die: A Novel of Redemption* (New York: HarperCollins, 1998).
2. Gabor Maté, *Scattered Minds: The Origins and Healing of Attention Deficit Disorder* (New York: Avery, 1999).

Chapter 9: Fitting In and Feeling Left Out

1. Stephen W. Porges, *The Polyvagal Theory: Neurophysiological Foundations of Emotions, Attachment, Communication, and Self-Regulation* (New York: Norton, 2011).
2. Brené Brown, *Braving the Wilderness: The Quest for True Belonging and the Courage to Stand Alone* (New York: Random House, 2017).

INDEX

ABOUT THE AUTHOR

Kati Morton is widely recognized as a leading mental health advocate and educator. She holds a master's in clinical psychology and is a licensed marriage and family therapist. She has a passion for education and empowerment and shares helpful insights through her YouTube channel. Kati is the author of two books, *Are u ok?* and *Traumatized*. She hopes that by speaking candidly about mental health and encouraging her viewers to reach out to get the support they need, we can remove the stigma associated with getting help.

RAISING READERS

Books Build Bright Futures

Thank you for reading this book and for being a reader of books in general. We are so grateful to share being part of a community of readers with you, and we hope you will join us in passing our love of books on to the next generation of readers.

Did you know that reading for enjoyment is the single biggest predictor of a child's future happiness and success?

More than family circumstances, parents' educational background, or income, reading impacts a child's future academic performance, emotional well-being, communication skills, economic security, ambition, and happiness.

Studies show that kids reading for enjoyment in the US is in rapid decline:

- In 2012, 53% of 9-year-olds read almost every day. Just 10 years later, in 2022, the number had fallen to 39%.
- In 2012, 27% of 13-year-olds read for fun daily. By 2023, that number was just 14%.

Together, we can commit to **Raising Readers** and change this trend. How?

- Read to children in your life daily.
- Model reading as a fun activity.
- Reduce screen time.
- Start a family, school, or community book club.
- Visit bookstores and libraries regularly.
- Listen to audiobooks.
- Read the book before you see the movie.
- Encourage your child to read aloud to a pet or stuffed animal.
- Give books as gifts.
- Donate books to families and communities in need.

BOB1217

Books build bright futures, and **Raising Readers** is our shared responsibility.

For more information, visit **JoinRaisingReaders.com**

Sources: National Endowment for the Arts, National Assessment of Educational Progress, WorldBookDay.org, Nielsen BookData's 2023 "Understanding the Children's Book Consumer"